1 and 2 Timothy, Titus

Keeping the Faith

I have fought the good fight, I have finished the race,
I have kept the faith.
2 Timothy 4:7

By A. C. Mueller

CONCORDIA PUBLISHING HOUSE · SAINT LOUIS

Written by A.C. Mueller

Edited by Tim Rake

Scripture quotations are from The Holy Bible, English Standard Version®, copyright © 2001 by Crossway Bibles, a publishing ministry of Good News Publishers, Wheaton, Illinois. Used by permission. All rights reserved.

The quotations from the Lutheran Confessions in this publication are from *Concordia: The Lutheran Confessions*, second edition, copyright © 2006 Concordia Publishing House. All rights reserved.

The quotation from Martin Luther in Lesson 13 is taken from *Luther's Small Catechism with Explanation*, copyright © 1986, 1991, 2005 Concordia Publishing House, p. 24.

This publication may be available in braille, in large print, or on cassette tape for the visually impaired. Please allow 8 to 12 weeks for delivery. Write to Lutheran Blind Mission, 7550 Watson Road, St. Louis, MO 63119-4409; call toll-free 1-888-215-2455; or visit the Web site: www.blindmission.org.

1 2 3 4 5 6 7 8 9 10   15 14 13 12 11 10 09 08 07 06

Contents

History	Date (AD)	1 and 2 Timothy, Titus
Descent of the Holy Spirit in Jerusalem (Acts 2)	ca. 30	
Martyrdom of Stephen (Acts 6:8–8:1)	32	Paul's conversion and Baptism (Acts 9:1–19; 22:1–16)
Caligula Roman Emperor	37–41	
Claudius Roman Emperor	41–54	
	46–48	Paul's first missionary journey
Apostolic council in Jerusalem (Acts 15)	49–52	Paul's second missionary journey
	53–57	Paul's third missionary journey
Nero Roman Emperor	54–68	
Martyrdom of James the Just	60–62	Paul under house arrest in Rome
	62–67	Paul's fourth missionary journey
Rome burns; Nero begins four-year persecution of Christians	July 9, 64	
	64–65	Paul writes 1 Timothy (1:1–2) and Titus (1:1–4)
	67	Paul imprisoned and chained in a dungeon by Nero; writes 2 Timothy (1:1–2)
Peter crucified upside down in Rome	67–68	Paul beheaded in Rome
Jerusalem captured and temple destroyed	70	
Construction begins on Roman Colosseum	71	

An Outline of 1 Timothy

This first of the Pastoral Epistles shows us that God blesses His Church through the Office of the Holy Ministry. Jesus Christ established this office to carry out the public ministry of the Gospel, which brings salvation to the whole world. Therefore, it bears a divine stamp of authority and power that is exercised through preaching and teaching, administration of the Sacraments, and overseeing the congregation. Because of this, the pastoral office is shaped, directed, and determined not by people but by Jesus Christ in accordance with the Gospel. Here is a basic outline.

I.   Salutation (1:1–2)
II. The charge concerning false teachers (1:3–20)
     A. The charge to preserve the purity of the Gospel (1:3–11)
     B. Two examples (1:12–20)
II. Instructions concerning pastoral ministry (2:1–3:16)
     A. Public worship (2:1–15)
        1. The duty of prayer (2:1–7)
        2. The position of men in public worship (2:8–10)
        3. The position of women in public worship (2:11–15)
     B. The qualifications for public ministry (3:1–13)
        1. Overseers (or pastors) (3:1–7)
        2. Deacons (3:8–13)
        3. The center and substance of public ministry (3:14–16)
III. Opposing false teachers (4:1–16)
     A. False teachers described (4:1–5)
     B. The pastor's work against false teachers (4:6–16)
IV. Pastoral ministry with various groups (5–6:2)
     A. Older and younger, widows, elders, and slaves (5:1–25)
     B. Concluding exhortations (6:3–19)
     C. Reiteration of charge (6:20–21)

An Outline of 2 Timothy

In this final letter before his execution under Nero, Paul writes to encourage Timothy, his protégé, to carry on the good fight of faith in the Gospel ministry. He reminds him that God's grace alone is the source of his power. While the Church and her ministers face persecution in this world and labor with much weakness, Christ will see to the victory of the Gospel. Because of this, Christ's ministers have the divine resources to keep the faith, even as Paul himself did.

I.   Introduction (1:1–4)
II. Encouragement for the pastor (1:5–18)
     A. God's gifts (1:5–7)
     B. God's faithfulness (1:6–12)
     C. The apostolic example of suffering (1:13–18)
III. Instructions concerning pastoral ministry (2:1–26)
     A. The call to endure by the power of grace (2:1–13)
     B. Avoiding errorists (2:14–26)
IV. Keeping the faith in the last days (3:1–17)
     A. The temptations (3:1–9)
     B. The means of grace (3:10–17)
V.   The final charge to keep the faith (4:1–8)
VI. The last words of one who has kept the faith (4:9–22)

An Outline of Titus

Like 1 Timothy, Titus is written to aid a pastor charged with overseeing the life and ministry of a young church planted by Paul. Titus' work is especially important because the devil is working to overthrow the Gospel through false teachers. This epistle reminds us that preserving and proclaiming the Gospel are twin duties that are vital to keeping the faith.

I.   Salutation (1:1–4)
II. The pastoral ministry (1:5–9)
   A. The necessity of pastors (1:5)
   B. The necessary qualities of pastors (1:6–9)
III. Opposing false teachers (1:10–16)
IV. The duties of pastoral ministry (2:1–15)
   A. Ministering to various groups (2:1–10)
   B. The Gospel basis of Christian living (2:11–14)
   C. The pastor's duty to minister the Gospel (2:15)
V.   Exhortation to Christian conduct (3:1–8)
VI. A reminder to oppose error (3:9–11)
VII. Conclusion (3:12–15)

Introduction to 1 and 2 Timothy and Titus

These three letters by Paul are often called the Pastoral Epistles because they address issues concerning the Office of the Holy Ministry or the pastoral office. They are the final three letters of Paul, and in them we are given a crucial understanding of the nature, character, and work of the Gospel ministry.

Paul is aware that his ministry is coming to a close and is concerned about the future of the Church. He is led by the Holy Spirit to give divine counsel to those who will succeed him in order that the Gospel and its ministry will continue just as he received them from the Lord. And through these divinely inspired words, he prepares every generation that follows to maintain faithfulness to the Lord and keep the faith.

Laypeople may be tempted to think that these letters do not concern them. Nothing could be farther from the truth. Understanding just what the will of our Lord is regarding the work of ministers will help them to be not only humble and grateful recipients of their pastors' service but genuinely useful assistants and friends to them.

Lesson 1

The Pastoral Epistles

The two letters of Paul to Timothy and the one to Titus are called the Pastoral Epistles because they were addressed to two young pastors. The apostle wished to give his faithful helpers special counsel for their work in the ministry. Yet these were written also for the benefit of all Christians and set forth important truths for godly living.

The First Epistle to Timothy

The Book of Acts and the epistles of Paul give a good picture of Timothy's life and work. For many years, he was a close friend and loyal companion of Paul. His home was at Lystra, a town of Asia Minor, where Paul preached the Gospel on his first missionary journey (Acts 14:8). His father was a Greek, but he had a Jewish mother, who along with his grandmother instructed him in the Old Testament Scriptures (2 Timothy 3:15). Timothy and his mother evidently became Christians when Paul preached the Gospel in Lystra (1 Timothy 1:2; 2 Timothy 1:5). When the apostle returned on his second journey, Timothy was recommended to him as a capable assistant (Acts 16:1). Timothy helped Paul greatly, and he rendered valuable service to the congregation that Paul founded but had to leave after a brief stay. During Paul's first imprisonment in Rome, Timothy visited him but then seems to have gone to Ephesus, where the apostle joined him after his release in AD 63. This was a difficult field, especially since false teachers were causing much trouble in the congregation (Acts 20:29–30). Paul departed for Macedonia and left Timothy in charge of the work in Ephesus. In order to help and encourage his faithful young friend, Paul wrote his first letter to Timothy from Macedonia, about AD 64 or 65.

1. Based on the following passages, describe Timothy's life and character: Acts 16:1–3; 17:14, 15; 18:5; 19:22; 2 Timothy 1:5; 3:15;

Philippians 2:19–23; 1 Thessalonians 1:1; 2 Thessalonians 1; 1 Corinthians 16:10; 2 Corinthians 1:1; Romans 16:21; Colossians 1:1.

2. How does Paul address Timothy in 1 Timothy 1:1–3 and 2 Timothy 1:1–5?

The Second Epistle to Timothy

This epistle is Paul's last, written shortly before his death in AD 67 or 68. After his release from his first imprisonment (AD 63), he seems to have visited Asia Minor, Macedonia, and Greece and may have gone as far west as Spain (Romans 15:24). At that time, Nero was already persecuting the Christians. Paul was arrested and taken to Rome, where he was imprisoned a second time. There, awaiting martyrdom, he wrote once more to Timothy and asked him to come to Rome as soon as possible (2 Timothy 4:9, 13, 21). Tradition says that he arrived in time to witness the apostle's execution and that he himself suffered a martyr's death at Ephesus some years later.

3. How is the tone of this letter altogether different from that of Paul's letters written during his first imprisonment when he was certain of being set free (Philippians 2:24; 1:25; Philemon 22; 2 Timothy 4:6, 16)?

4. What longing did Paul express at this time (2 Timothy 1:4; 4:9, 21)?

The Epistle to Titus

Titus was another faithful coworker of the apostle. We know very little about him. Luke does not mention him in the Book of Acts. He is first mentioned in Galatians 2:3, where Paul speaks of him as a Gentile Christian whom he refused to circumcise because the Judaizers demanded this rite as necessary for salvation. He accompanies Paul to Jerusalem for the apostolic council (Acts 15). Titus is mentioned frequently in Paul's Second Epistle to the Corinthians. He joined Paul on his third missionary journey and evidently delivered Paul's Second Epistle to the Corinthians. We do not know what Titus did during the apostle's first imprisonment. Apparently, after leaving Rome en route to Asia Minor, Paul stopped briefly at the island of Crete and with Titus's help founded some congregations (Titus 1:5, 12). He left Titus in charge of this difficult field, and from Macedonia he sent Titus this personal letter about the time he wrote his first epistle to Timothy. After fulfilling his work and placing others in charge of the churches on Crete, Titus was to join Paul at Nicopolis (3:12). Later he was sent to preach the Gospel in Dalmatia (2 Timothy 4:10). Tradition says Titus died on the island of Crete at the age of ninety-four.

5. What do we learn about Titus in 2 Corinthians 2:13; 7:6, 7, 13–15; 8:16–18, 23; 12:18?

6. How is Titus addressed in Titus 1:4? What was his special task in verse 5?

7. How does Paul describe the Cretans in 1:12?

8. Why are God's instructions to pastors of importance to all believers?

In Closing

Encourage participants to begin the following activities:
- Begin to familiarize yourself with Paul's missionary journeys by reading Acts 13:4–21:7.
- In preparation for the next session, read 1 Timothy 1.

Close with prayer.

Lesson 2

The Firm Foundation of Our Faith

The Pastoral Epistles stress the importance of pure doctrine. The reason for that is that there were teachers in those days who claimed that they were teaching a much better way of salvation and the Christian life than the apostles, whose doctrine was rooted in the Gospel. But by their impure doctrine, these false teachers were trying to rob Christians of their faith. The same thing is happening in many churches today. People are asked to believe many things that are contrary to God's Word. Therefore, in order that we may not lose our faith, it is of greatest importance that we know and cling to the true doctrines of the Bible.

Doctrines That Make Faith Impossible

Read 1 Timothy 1:1–7. On his third missionary journey, Paul had built up a strong Christian congregation in Ephesus, which was soundly indoctrinated in the Word of God. But the apostle knew that Satan would soon try to lead those believers away from the truth by sending false teachers into their midst (Acts 20:29–30). When Timothy became pastor of that church, he discovered that Paul's prophecy had come true. Some men in Ephesus were actually teaching other doctrines, matters that were contrary to the truths Paul had taught. These people were indeed using the Bible, but they employed it in the wrong way. Some read into the Scriptures things that were not there. They invented myths and legendary stories about the Old Testament saints, and they attached great importance to the genealogies, or lists of names, raising all kinds of useless questions about them. Others claimed that they were teaching the true meaning and use of the Law, but they misunderstood its purpose altogether and therefore wasted their time with worthless disputes after the manner of the Jewish scribes. They taught that unless a man kept the Law he could not be saved, but they had not grasped that the Law demands love out of a pure heart and that only a believer can do what the Law requires.

9. What are some of the things that people hear from pulpits where God's Word is not taught in all its truth and purity?

10. How do some preachers reveal that they do not understand the Law of God?

The Only Way We Can Have Faith

Read 1 Timothy 1:8–15. The apostle had always taught that the Law cannot make man righteous before God. It is, of course, God's Word, and therefore it is to serve a good and necessary purpose. It shows men that they are sinners, and it warns them that God will punish them for their sins. Ungodly people must have the Law preached to them to show them the need of a Savior and to lead them to repentance. But the Law cannot bestow upon them the righteousness of faith. For this purpose, God has given us His glorious Gospel. Paul's own example shows what the Gospel is able to do. Before his conversion, the apostle had grievously offended God, even though he had tried earnestly to live according to the Law. But when the Lord revealed His mercy and grace to Paul and assured him of the forgiveness of his sins, the apostle became a different man. The Gospel worked faith in his heart and united him with his Savior. What joy and comfort it was for him that Jesus had come into the world to save even such great sinners as he realized he had been! Paul believed this Gospel with all his heart, and he wanted no other doctrine preached for the salvation of men. By means of this sound doctrine that Paul had taught at Lystra, Timothy had also come to faith (v. 2).

11. What is the threefold use of the Law?

12. How does Paul's case prove that the Law cannot make a person righteous?

13. Why did he consider himself to have been the greatest of sinners (Acts 9:1–2)?

14. Why is 1 Timothy 1:15 one of the most comforting passages of the Bible? Why may we safely base our faith upon the Gospel?

The Practical Value of a Strong Faith

Read verses 16–20. The Gospel changed the whole aim and course of Paul's life. By the mercy of God, the former enemy of Jesus and the Church became one of the greatest preachers of the Gospel and, by living a godly life, he served his fellow men as a pattern of faith and godliness. Paul's chief aim was to make God in Christ known to all people, so that all might honor and glorify Him as the only God and their eternal King. Timothy, too, lived the life of a true believer. The apostle urged him to continue on the way of godliness, to fight against sin and error, and to cling firmly to the doctrine of faith. The assurance that Christ has forgiven our sins and made us children of God enables us at all times to walk before God with a good conscience. As long as faith rules in our hearts, our sins may not rise up to condemn us, and we need not fear that God will punish us. However, we will not enjoy this peace with God if we grow careless and fall from faith. Paul reminds Timothy of two former church members in Ephesus who had to be excommunicated because they had made shipwrecks of their faith as a result of permitting the false teachers to influence them.

15. In what sense is the life of a Christian like warfare?

16. Of what value is a good conscience?

17. Why do some fall away after being confirmed?

18. How should the Church deal with members who have given offense by living ungodly lives or by teaching false doctrines (Matthew 18:15–17; 1 Corinthians 5:13; Titus 3:10)?

In Closing

Encourage participants to begin the following activities:
- Discuss how every Christian doctrine is tied to justification by God's grace through faith in Christ.
- In preparation for the next session, read 1 Timothy 2.

Close with prayer.

Lesson 3

The Christian in the House of God

Church services occupy an important place in the lives of believers. Christians regard the church as the house of God, where they meet with their fellow Christians for public worship and where they receive the blessings of God's Word, which strengthen and keep them in the faith. Those who truly appreciate the benefits of church services will not only be regular in their attendance but will also come in the right spirit and conduct themselves in a manner befitting the house of God. Paul shows what God expects of us when we are in church.

The Importance of Congregational Prayer

Read 1 Timothy 2:1–3, 8. Christians should pray often in their daily lives, at home, and wherever else they may be. But they should regard especially the church as their house of prayer and worship. Christians should attend the Divine Service in a prayerful and devotional spirit and take an active part in the prayers and the singing of the congregation. Paul makes a strong appeal to all Christians to engage in public prayer. He describes such prayers as supplications and petitions offered in the spirit of humility and reverence, in childlike confidence, and in grateful acknowledgment of God's blessings.

The apostle also tells us for whom we should pray: not only for ourselves, our loved ones, and our congregation, but also for all people. As surely as we are to love our neighbor as ourselves, it is likewise our duty to pray for all people. In particular, we should pray for our country and government. The welfare of every nation is bound up with its government. By praying for it, we not only render a great service to our country but also share in the good things that God bestows upon our land in answer to our prayers. When God grants peace and prosperity and preserves our nation from war and hard times, we have the opportunity to make an honest and comfortable living and the Church is able to do its work unhindered.

Finally, Paul tells us how we are to pray (v. 8). When he says that we should lift up holy hands, he is not referring to postures or gestures in prayer but to our hearts and lives. God will not hear us if sin still rules in our hearts. Our prayers will be in vain as long as we hate our neighbor or doubt God's promises in regard to prayer.

19. What rules for praying does Jesus give in John 16:23; Matthew 7:7–8; 8:2; 21:22?

20. Why is a person who is angry with someone unable to pray (Matthew 5:23–24; 6:12, 15)?

21. Why will God not hear the prayers of those who doubt His promises (James 1:6–7; 5:16)?

Taking the Message to Heart

Read verses 4–7. In these verses, Paul shows what should prompt us to pray for all people. He points to the glorious message of God that we are privileged to hear at every church service. This message tells us about God's love toward us and all people through His Son, Jesus Christ. The Gospel tells us that God's love embraces all people. He wants all to hear and believe His Word and be saved. In order to save sinful humankind, God sent His Son into the world. Jesus became man to be our substitute, and He served as the mediator between God and man by reconciling us to God by making full payment for our sins on the cross. Jesus' life and blood were the ransom by which He bought us free from sin and the power of Satan. In the blessed Gospel, God offers us His grace and eternal salvation through Christ, which becomes ours through the gift of faith. Therefore, we should faithfully hear the Gospel, take it to heart, and believe it. We should also remember that the Gospel is for all people and that God wants us to bring it to others.

22. Why is the preaching of the Gospel so very important in church services (Romans 10:17)?

23. How are we certain that Jesus has saved us?

24. Why should we be deeply concerned about the salvation of our neighbor?

Proper Conduct in Church Services

Read 1 Timothy 2:9–15. In this section, the apostle is speaking particularly of women, but his words apply also to churchgoers in general. There is a temptation to pay more attention to one's outward appearance than to the real purpose of public worship. The apostle does not forbid women to dress becomingly or to wear jewelry. But he does not want them to dress for public display, whereby they may draw the attention of other worshipers upon themselves or deprive their souls of the benefits of the church service. The same could be said of men or youth. God desires that Christians adorn themselves with good works as the fruits of faith.

Women have the same rights and privileges as far as the Gospel is concerned (Galatians 3:28), but they are not to assume leadership over men (1 Corinthians 14:34–35). They are not permitted to preach and teach in the public meetings of the congregation. At creation, the Lord established woman's position as subordinate to man. If God's arrangement is ignored, the Church is sure to suffer harm. This is clear from the example of Eve who misled Adam into sin. If married, a woman's primary sphere of life and service is to her husband and children, just as a husband's duties are completed for wife and child in loving respect and self-sacrifice (Ephesians 5:22–30).

25. How is a woman's position explained in 1 Corinthians 14:34–35; Ephesians 5:22; Colossians 3:18; 1 Peter 3:1?

26. Why should women not be allowed to serve as pastors? Whom are women permitted to teach (2 Timothy 1:5; Titus 2:3–4)?

27. How does Christianity truly elevate womanhood (Galatians 3:28)?

In Closing

Encourage participants to begin the following activities:
• Read 1 Peter 3:1–12 and consider how husbands and wives should relate to one another and how this is an occasion to bear witness to the Gospel.
• In preparation for the next session, read 1 Timothy 3.

Close with prayer.

Lesson 4

Serving the Lord in the Church

What is the most important work of the Church? Who is responsible for the carrying out of the Church's program? Some people want to enjoy the privileges and benefits of church membership, but they show no willingness to have a share in the work of the Church. God wants everything in the Church to be well regulated and conducted in an orderly and efficient manner. Therefore, Paul gave Timothy definite instructions on how every congregation should fulfill its obligations and manage its affairs.

Qualifications of a Pastor

Read 1 Timothy 3:1–7 and see also Titus 1:6–9. The Office of the Ministry is the highest office in the Church. In fact, it is the only office that God has established for every congregation (Acts 20:28; 1 Timothy 5:17). Those who serve in the ministry have a difficult task to perform, and they bear a heavy responsibility (Hebrews 13:17). Because no other work is more important for the people's welfare, St. Paul wants the congregations to call as their pastors only men (adult males) who have the proper qualifications.

A pastor should, first of all, be a devout Christian and have a good character and reputation. The virtues that are required of all Christians should be especially noticeable in pastors, because they are to serve as good examples to their flocks. If their conduct is bad, people will not be inclined to listen to their message. A pastor should, therefore, keep himself under control and not allow himself to be ruled by sinful desires and habits, such as intemperance, bad temper, greed, or pride. If he is married and has children, he should conduct his home in an exemplary Christian manner and lead his family to live a pure and godly life. In general, a pastor should have the welfare of his flock and of all people at heart and should be able to serve them by word and deed. For that reason a newly converted person (recent convert), who has not yet been able to prove that he is a strong Christian, should not be called into the ministry. Moreover, a person must also have certain ministerial gifts, without which he cannot serve as a pastor. He must have the ability to teach and preach the Word of God and to apply it to the needs of his flock. For this reason he also needs to be well trained for his work and to acquire a sound and thorough knowledge of the Holy Scriptures (Titus 1:9).

28. Discuss the lists of qualifications for pastors in 1 Timothy 3 and Titus 1:6–9.

29. What specific duties of pastors are indicated in 1 Timothy 4:6, 12–16; 2 Timothy 2:15, 24–26; 4:2; Titus 1:11; 2:1, 7?

30. Why should pastors be good examples to their flocks?

31. What do church members owe to their pastors (1 Timothy 5:17)?

Lay Workers Needed to Assist the Pastor

Read 1 Timothy 3:8–13. In order to give the apostles and elders (pastors) more time for preaching and teaching, the early Christian Church assigned certain duties, such as visiting the sick and caring for the poor, to qualified and consecrated lay workers, known as deacons (Acts 6:1–6). Regardless of whether these men gave all or only part of their time to the Church, they had to be sound in faith and Christian knowledge and able to perform their assigned tasks. It was also very important that they should live exemplary lives at home as well as in public. If they were careless in their conduct or showed that they were out for personal gain and glory, some of those whom they served might take offense and leave the Church. In verse 11, the apostle gives similar directions to female workers (deaconesses). They had to look after the needs of the female members. These had to be particularly on their guard not to carry gossip from house to house or say things that might cause trouble in the congregations. Therefore, they needed a good measure of sincerity, faithfulness, and sound judgment. Such service would help them to grow in Christian knowledge and experience, and God promised graciously to reward them for their good works (v. 13).

32. What offices have our congregations established to assist the pastors in their work? What kind of persons should be chosen for these duties?

33. Why should every church member pay close attention to his conduct at home and in public?

Willing and Joyful Service

Read verses 14–16. Paul considered the work of the Church so important that he did not wait until he could talk these matters over personally with Timothy. He put his instructions down in writing so that they would also be available to the believers of all times. The work that is done in and through the Church is far different from all other kinds of activity among people, because the Church is the house of God in which the living God rules and dwells. The Church is a pillar and buttress of truth, because it has the Word of God, the only truth that makes us wise unto salvation. God has committed to the Church the blessed Gospel, which is to be preached to all people. The Gospel is given in the form of a hymn (v. 16) and is called a divine mystery, something that human beings could not know if God had not revealed it. By means of the Gospel, God tells us what He has done for our salvation. He had His Son become man in order to redeem us from sin. All who believe in Jesus have forgiveness of sins. The exalted Jesus has His Gospel preached through His Church to all the world, so that people may be brought to faith and share in His heavenly glory. We have and enjoy this precious Gospel, and we should be eager to share it with others.

34. Why should our house of worship be especially dear to our hearts?

35. Why should we be very grateful for having the pure Gospel?

In Closing

Encourage participants to begin the following activities:

• Discuss how participants see the image of Christ in the qualifications for the pastoral office given in 1 Timothy 3.

• Discuss 1 Timothy 3:16 and how the person and work of Christ for us are to be the focus of the Divine Service.

• In preparation for the next session, read 1 Timothy 4.

Close with prayer.

Lesson 5

Godliness in Everyday Life

Why do some people derive very little benefit from their membership in the Church? Evidently they do not let the Gospel take a firm hold of their hearts and permit its influence to reach out into their daily lives. With some people, faith in Christ seems to be nothing more than a Sunday morning affair. During the week, they lay it aside and live just as the world does. The Christianity they profess is a sham. Paul shows that a believer practices his or her faith every day of his or her life.

The Way to Enjoy God's Gifts

Read 1 Timothy 4:1–5. The people who try to spoil the good things in life for us are those who want us to follow their wisdom instead of the Word of God. Paul warns Timothy and all believers against these false leaders. When people set up all kinds of rules of life by which they think they can make the world better and even claim divine authority for their pet notions, they are dangerous deceivers and are spreading "teachings of demons" (v. 1). They are skillful in using pious phrases, but their teachings leave people with a bad conscience. Paul's prophecy has come true; there have been many who caused disturbances in the Church with their human-made doctrines. For instance, how often has it been claimed, even by church bodies, that marriage is sinful or that a Christian may not use certain kinds of food? Some have insisted that a person must deny himself natural and created blessings to please God and go to heaven. But what does the Bible say about the things of this life? It teaches plainly that God has given them to us for our welfare and enjoyment. To be sure, we are not to use them in a sinful manner, as unbelievers often do. The Christian knows that God has created these things for his use and benefit. He or she is deeply grateful to God for these gifts and uses them in a God-pleasing manner to His glory. Thus marriage is a divine institution, and therefore it must serve the good of humankind (Genesis 2:18; Hebrews 13:4). They also know that God causes the earth to bring forth food for their sustenance (Genesis 1:29). Everything that is wholesome for the body may be eaten with a good conscience, especially when it is received with prayer and thanksgiving (Matthew 6:11; Fourth Petition of the Lord's Prayer).

36. What human-made rules have churches set up as means for obtaining salvation and blessing from God?

37. What does 1 Timothy 4:4 teach concerning the use of alcoholic beverages? Does the New Testament forbid the use of any kind of food or drink (Colossians 2:16; 1 Corinthians 10:31)?

38. Describe the character of false teachers, and note what the Word of God identifies as the source of their error. What effect do human restrictions have upon people's consciences?

The Christian's Estimate of Values

Read 1 Timothy 4:6–11. Paul wants believers to have good judgment and a sound understanding of values. The good doctrine, which only the Bible can teach, is the Gospel, and its goodness is the blessing of salvation that it brings. Therefore, our chief concern should be to grow in the knowledge of God's Word and become strong in the faith. The soul constantly needs nourishment, and it will be well nourished if we make diligent use of the Holy Scriptures. The more firmly we are grounded in the Word of God, the easier it will be for us to recognize and resist the foolish and dangerous doctrines of men. Maintaining physical health is not forbidden, of course, but no amount or kind of bodily discipline will improve upon the grace of God or make us more righteous and holy in God's sight. Compared with the value of a godly life, all things pertaining to the body are of minor importance. But true godliness, which includes both faith and a sanctified life, promises spiritual life both now (life under the cross lived in humility and weakness) and in eternity (life in resurrection triumph lived in power and glory). As long as we live a life of faith, we have spiritual life, which finally is realized as eternal life in heaven. Believers may always be sure of this because they have God's promise. Therefore, they should daily exercise themselves unto godliness and put their trust in the living God, regardless of what they have to do or suffer in this world.

39. Why is it important that we are nourished with God's Word?

40. How do some people show that the care of their bodies means more to them than that of their souls?

41. What does "some value" (v. 8) mean? What is godliness?

Living with a Purpose

Read verses 12–16. As a Christian, but especially as a pastor, Timothy had an important position to fill in the world (v. 11). A believer's entire conduct should indicate that he or she is a child of God. In order to keep one's spiritual life on a high plane, the believer should devote time to the study of the Word of God. This is particularly true of the pastor. He should seek to obtain a thorough knowledge of all doctrines of Scripture and learn to apply them to his life. God bestows priceless spiritual gifts upon us in Baptism and by means of the Word, which we read and hear. The pastor has in the same way received through the Word of God a special gift and enablement from God to shepherd God's people. If we neglect spiritual gifts, we may lose them.

42. Why is it just as important for the pastor to live out the Gospel among God's people?

43. What spiritual gift is imparted to those in the pastoral office?

44. Why should the pastor devote his time to the study and meditation of Scripture? What demands or expectations do church members sometimes have that fail to recognize this priority or that discourage the pastor from doing so?

45. How does the pastor's devotion to God's Word benefit the Church? How is this an example for all Christians?

In Closing

Encourage participants to begin the following activities:
- Read John 21:15–19 and 1 Peter 5:1–4, and discuss briefly the chief duty of pastors.
- Read Luke 10:16, and note the authority Jesus gives to those whom He sends to minister in His name.
- In preparation for the next session, read 1 Timothy 5.

Close with prayer.

Lesson 6

Responsibilities Toward Others

Human beings are dependent upon one another for their common welfare. As members of human society, we have certain responsibilities toward other persons and are expected to contribute our share to the well-being of others. Paul shows very clearly that we are not in this world merely for our own sake. God has put us here to live useful lives in the service of our neighbor.

Encouraging Others to Live Godly Lives

Read 1 Timothy 5:1–7. As a pastor, Timothy had to give close attention to the lives of all his church members regardless of their age or sex. It sometimes happens that a believer becomes careless and permits the sinful flesh to gain control. The best service that a fellow Christian can render a person who has fallen into a sin is to warn him or her and to admonish him or her to repent (Matthew 18:15; Galatians 6:1, 2; James 5:19–20). In fact, it is our Christian duty that we do all we can to keep our brother or sister from losing his or her faith. It is not easy to tell another person that he or she has done wrong and that he or she should repent. However, we should at all times have the spiritual welfare of our fellow Christians at heart and deal with them in brotherly love. It is particularly important that believers watch their conduct in their homes and show the right Christian attitude toward their relatives, friends, neighbors, and co-workers. On the other hand, when a person stands alone in the world, he or she should not consider himself or herself forsaken by God or seek to support himself or herself in a sinful manner. He or she should be encouraged to rely upon God and make all his wants known to the Lord in prayer.

46. What is our Christian duty when we see someone committing a sin (Matthew 18:15–17)? Why should we not approach such a person in a superior or condemning manner?

47. Why should we show sympathy and kindness especially to widows and older people who are left alone and especially our own parents?

Living Useful Lives

Read 1 Timothy 5:8–16. As long as a person is able to support himself or herself, he or she should not remain idle and depend on others for a living. God wants everyone to earn his or her own living by honest labor and also provide for those who are dependent upon his or her support. A person who has a family, aged parents and grand-parents, or other relatives who cannot supply their own needs has the obligation to provide for them according to his or her ability. Even non-Christian people recognize this natural law. Therefore, if a church member neglects to take care of his or her dependents, he or she contradicts his or her faith. Paul says he or she "is worse than an unbeliever" (v. 8). On the other hand, the apostle teaches that only a person who is not able to earn his or her own living is entitled to the support of others. The early Christians seem to have kept special lists of needy persons, and the congregations took care of them if they had no other means of support. The circumstances in which most widows found themselves were pitiful, because it was much harder in those days for them to find employment. In the case of younger women, they could find little to do, and these were in danger of spending their time unproductively. The only way in which to remedy that situation in those days was to compel the young widows to try to support them-selves or to seek another marriage. But the apostle did not want them to marry non-Christian men who might win them away from Christ. The home always offers a woman ample opportunity to serve God and others with all kinds of necessary good works. Her position as a wife and mother is also her best safeguard against the temptations of the devil. In general, God has established the rule that every person who is able to support himself or herself and his or her dependents is obliged to do so, but that the Church is to take care of those who lack all other means of support.

48. Why should every person seek to be regularly employed? What should be taken into consideration when one is choosing his life work (John 15:1–8; Romans 12:17b; 2 Corinthians 8:21)?

49. Why does the Bible emphasize the home life of believers?

A Christian's Attitude toward His Pastor

Read 1 Timothy 5:17–25. God wants us to respect and honor those who preach and teach the Word of God. We should regard them as dealing with us in God's stead for the welfare of our souls. They are entitled to a salary adequate for their needs and a fair compensation for their labors as evidence of our appreciation of their service to us. We should guard against making unkind or slanderous remarks about our pastors. Nothing will undermine their usefulness more than vicious gossip that is spread about them. Therefore, we should not let others raise evil charges against them. However, when it is evident that a pastor has sinned, he must be admonished. If he remains impenitent, he is not to be tolerated in the congregation; otherwise the members become guilty of his sin. When such conditions arise, Christians should act in fairness and not show partiality toward any person. Finally, the apostle says that the Christian should strive to keep his or her life pure by doing the right thing at all times. He or she should make proper use of the means that God has given for the preservation of his or her health.

50. When do we show that we honor our pastors and teachers (Hebrews 13:17; 1 Thessalonians 5:12–13; Galatians 6:6; 1 Corinthians 9:14)?

51. How should we act when we hear our pastors unjustly criticized and slandered?

In Closing

Encourage participants to begin the following activities:
- Read Matthew 25:31–46, and discuss how what we learn about the treatment of others from this parable may apply especially to how we treat pastors.
- In preparation for the next session, read 1 Timothy 6.

Close with prayer.

Lesson 7

Christian Stewardship

Remarkably, the Bible has much to say about riches, money, and property and their use. It speaks of wealth as one of the gravest dangers to faith, and yet some of the great saints of the Bible were very rich. How then should Christians regard earthly possessions so that they may not harm their souls? As Paul shows in our text, a Christian should consider himself or herself at all times merely a steward of talents and property that God has loaned to him or her for a season. One means by which we may glorify God on earth is Christian stewardship.

The Stewardship of Service

Read 1 Timothy 6:1–5. A large number of Christians in the Early Church were slaves. This shouldn't surprise us because the Roman Empire had a large slave population, and the Gospel did more than anything else to ease their burdens. As a rule, non-Christian masters did not object to their servants becoming Christians, because they noticed that this improved their conduct and service. Paul reminds the Christian slaves that they must be on their guard not to turn their masters against the Gospel by unfaithfulness or ungodly conduct. Instead, they should by an exemplary life try to win them for Christ. On the other hand, those slaves who had Christian masters were very fortunate. Their lot should have been somewhat easier and more tolerable, since Christians naturally treated their servants kindly. However, since slaves and masters were equal in the Church and considered one another brethren (Galatians 3:28), there was danger that slaves might not show their masters the respect and obedience they owed them. Paul wanted the servants to render willing and loving service to their masters. In fact, he admonishes all Christians to walk the way of godliness and to be obedient to the wholesome words of

Jesus. Such a God-pleasing life is not possible if a believer listens to evil-minded people who set forth their personal advantages and earthly gain as the chief aim of life.

52. Discuss slavery in Roman times and what the Bible teaches regarding its practice.

53. Why should a Christian be very careful about his conduct while at work? How may we make our occupation a field for Christian service?

54. What is meant by stewardship of time and talents?

The Stewardship of Possessions

Read verses 6–10 and 17–19. In the first section, Paul speaks to those who want to be rich. He warns them against the dangers of covetousness and admonishes them to be content with the share of temporal wealth that God has given them. As long as a person's heart is ruled by greed and discontent, he or she cannot live as a child of God. The love of money is sinful and harmful. When people yield to a craving for wealth, they easily fall into temptations to enrich themselves by sinful means. Faith cannot remain in the heart of a person who worships mammon (Matthew 6:24). The reward of such unholy desires is always sorrow and disappointment. When a covetous person dies, he loses not only his or her treasures but also his or her soul.

But it is altogether different with the believer who does not hang his or her heart on perishable things. As long as a Christian has food and clothing, the necessary things of life, he or she is happy and content. In fact, God has given us much more than we actually need for ourselves. The Lord sometimes bestows a great amount of earthly goods on some Christians in order to test their faith and enable them to be of greater service to others. In 1 Timothy 6:17–19, the apostle shows how Christians should regard and use their possessions. He warns them not to become puffed up because of their wealth and not to despise others. They should not make a god of their possessions but should rely only upon the Lord as the giver of all good things, appreciate His gifts, and consider how they may serve God best as His stewards. If they use their possessions to the glory of God and for the benefit of their neighbors in need, they will grow rich in good works, which God has promised to reward in heaven.

55. How much does a person need to live a normal and happy life? Why is it foolish and sinful to spend one's life trying to become rich?

56. Why does Paul call the love of money the root of all evil?

The Stewardship of Faith

Read verses 11–16. An important rule for the believer is to flee all temptations to sin and devote himself or herself entirely to the cultivation of Christian virtues, which are the fruits of faith. By following after the things that please God, the Christian proves that he or she is a child of God. The believer has to wage a constant and difficult war against sin, the devil, and the flesh. However, this is a good and necessary fight, which serves to make the child of God stronger in the faith and finally leads to victory. By faith, the believer remains in possession of the eternal life to which God has called him or her and gives evidence of this spiritual life through daily conduct and by confessing the faith. Christ Himself is the perfect example. He teaches us to proclaim the truth fearlessly before people. The Gospel is the means by which the Holy Spirit makes people spiritually alive and active. It enables the believer to walk in the ways of God's commandments and to live confidently until the return of Christ. A Christian's chief desire is to live to the glory of the blessed Savior, the King of kings and Lord of lords, and to receive eternal life from Him.

57. What does it mean to fight the good fight of faith? How did Paul illustrate this in his own life?

58. Why should we think of the confession we made on the day of our confirmation?

In Closing

Encourage participants to begin the following activities:

- Read the following passages from Proverbs and discuss what they teach about wealth in the believer's life: 11:4, 28; 13:7; 19:14; 22:4, 16; 23:5; 30:8.
- In preparation for the next session, read 2 Timothy 1.

Close with prayer.

Lesson 8

Be Not Ashamed of Your Faith

When Paul wrote his Second Letter to Timothy, he was an old man, and he was lying in a prison cell awaiting a martyr's death. After Paul was gone, would others show the same love for the Gospel and work with the same zeal to have it spread as he had done? The apostle had learned by bitter experience that there were some on whom he could not depend. When they felt that their lives were in danger, they did not want others to regard them as Christians. But it comforted him to know that not all his friends were like that. Timothy certainly had proved that he was not ashamed of his faith.

A Young Man with a Splendid Record

Read 2 Timothy 1:1–8. The apostle had become more closely attached to Timothy than to any other of his other co-workers. During all the years that Paul had known him, Timothy had given a good account of himself as a sincere and consecrated Christian. The training and the instruction in the Scriptures that he had received from his devout mother, Eunice, and grandmother, Lois, had borne rich fruits in his later life. He had showed that he was not ashamed of his faith and of having been associated with the apostle whom the enemies of the Gospel sought to kill. No wonder Paul loved his much younger friend with great affection. Timothy's loyalty and sincerity filled Paul's heart with joy and thanksgiving to God (Philippians 2:19–22). What deep emotions he must have felt as he was writing his farewell message to his friend in faraway Ephesus! He could not forget Timothy's tears the last time they had parted. The great apostle never failed to include his faithful helper in his daily prayers. He knew what problems and dangers Timothy was facing as a pastor and as a Christian. Timothy had already suffered much for the sake of the Gospel, but he had remained faithful to the Lord and His apostle. Paul did not want his young friend to become discouraged or fear their enemies. He encouraged him faithfully to keep on using the splendid gifts God had given him, bravely to confess his faith before men, and patiently to endure afflictions and persecution.

59. Why is it a great blessing to grow up in a godly home?

60. What are the advantages of being a believer from early childhood?

61. Why should we daily remember our relatives and friends in our prayers?

62. When do we have a "sincere faith" (2 Timothy 1:5; 1 Timothy 1:5)?

The Heroic Faith of St. Paul

Read 2 Timothy 1:9–14. All the years that Paul had been a Christian, he had to suffer for the sake of the Gospel, perhaps more than any other person. Now he was a prisoner in Rome for the second time, and it seemed certain that soon he would be led to his death. But Paul was unafraid and did not complain about his hard lot. While in the dark dungeon, he thought of the many good things that he enjoyed as a believer. Why should he fear people or worry about the future since Jesus had redeemed his soul, called him to faith and eternal salvation, and assured him by the Gospel of a glorious resurrection and everlasting life in heaven (Romans 8:18, 38–39)? God had revealed

His love and mercy to Paul in a very special way by making him a preacher of the Gospel and the apostle and teacher of the Gentiles. He knew that neither suffering nor death could rob him of these blessings. His faith was firmly grounded on Jesus, and he was certain that the Lord would keep him in the faith unto his end. What a wonderfully strong faith and what a beautiful confession of faith in the darkest hour of trial (2 Timothy 1:12)! Paul was never ashamed of his faith, no matter how much he had to suffer on account of it. Oh, that we all had such a heroic faith (Philippians 1:21)!

63. When things are going bad for us, why should we not brood over our sufferings but think of what God has done for us?

64. Why should a believer at all times be certain that he or she will inherit eternal life?

65. Why should we never be ashamed of the Gospel (Romans 1:16)?

66. Why should we daily seek to grow stronger in faith? What means has God given us for this purpose?

Loyalty to the Brethren

Read 2 Timothy 1:15–18. Soon after his second imprisonment, Paul was brought to trial before Emperor Nero. He had been accused of being the teacher of a religion that was forbidden in the Roman Empire. At that time, it was a dangerous thing to be known as a

Christian or even to take sides with a person like Paul. Fearing that they might have to suffer imprisonment and death if they were seen in the apostle's company, some of Paul's former friends from Asia Minor hastily withdrew from him and tried to conceal the fact that they were Christians. Instead of helping and encouraging the apostle, they grieved his heart by their disloyalty. What was worse, in denying the apostle they denied Christ and showed that they had lost their faith. However, one friend of the apostle remained faithful and showed that he was a sincere Christian. Onesiphorus did all he could to comfort and relieve Paul in his distress. Although he seems to have had considerable difficulty finding the apostle, he was determined to help his beloved teacher. After a painstaking search, he found his friend and served him as best he could, just as he had formerly done in Ephesus. We do not know what had become of Onesiphorus when Paul wrote about him to Timothy. Perhaps Paul himself did not know, but he prayed that God would graciously reward Onesiphorus and his family for all the kindness they had bestowed upon him.

67. What is wrong with a church member who is ashamed of fellow Christians?

68. Why should we not consider our personal interests when our fellow Christians need our help?

69. How does God regard our service of love (Matthew 25:40)?

70. Do you know of any person whom you could cheer by a visit?

In Closing

Encourage participants to begin the following activities:

- Read Matthew 25:36–40, and discuss what special deeds of mercy are mentioned.
- In preparation for the next session, read 2 Timothy 2.

Close with prayer.

Lesson 9

Christian Warfare

What an inspiring sight to see a regiment of soldiers on parade, marching along while the band plays! Who would not be willing to exchange places with them then? But it is an altogether different matter when the soldiers are on the battlefield. The Bible pictures the Christian life as a constant struggle that the believer must wage against the enemies of his or her soul. It is a hard and long conflict. And, alas, how many give up, and some when it has barely begun! They dress up for the parade, but they do not want to fight. Our lesson shows what a serious business it is to be a Christian.

A Life of Self-Discipline

Read 2 Timothy 2:1–10. Timothy held a very difficult position in the city of Ephesus. His congregation was threatened by dangers from within, and the fires of persecution were being kindled against Christians. Paul did not want to see his young friend lose courage in fighting the Lord's battles. In order to be able to stand his ground, Timothy needed to be strong in the grace of God. It was also his duty to strengthen his fellow Christians, so that they would continue to fight bravely and ward off the attacks of the devil and the world. Timothy's past experiences had served to train him for more difficult tasks. He had become hardened by trials and sufferings, so that he was able to endure hardships for the sake of the Gospel. Paul encouraged him to face the problems of his Christian calling bravely. He should not be unduly concerned about the affairs of this life but, like a good soldier, strive to please the Captain whom he was serving. As an athlete who takes part in some contest has to play the game according to the rules, so Timothy should keep God's Word before him and order his life according to it. The "rule" is the Gospel and the grace of God. The false teachers Timothy faced boasted of righteousness by the Law.

They talked of works and various schemes of self-produced holiness. But Paul says ironically that this violates the "rule" of the Gospel, which is about faith, grace, and love. Again, a Christian pastor is like a farmer, who must work hard and long but finally can enjoy the fruits of his labors. Thus, the faithful pastor will successfully reach the goal of his ministry, which is to serve people with God's grace and gifts. Christ will reward His loyal servants (1 Peter 5:1–4). He gives them the strength and knowledge to carry on successful warfare. He has gone this same way before them, even into death, but He is alive, and by means of the Gospel He leads His people to victory. God's Word cannot be checked or bound by wicked people, even though those who proclaim it may be cast into prison or killed. Like Paul, every believer should gladly do his or her part and bring the needed sacrifices to help the Gospel win new victories and save people for eternal life.

71. How does a person become strong in the grace of God (2 Peter 3:18)?

72. In what respects does a Christian resemble a soldier (1 Timothy 6:12)? an athlete (1 Corinthians 9:24–27)? a farmer (1 Corinthians 9:10)?

73. What is the "rule" of pastoral ministry and Christian living?

God's Word Our Weapon

Read 2 Timothy 2:11–19. The Christian is not alone in his or her warfare against sin and evil. If Jesus, our great Captain, would not lead us and fight at our side, we would soon be lost. It should not be an irksome burden to live, fight, and die for Him, since He gave His life for us. Because He lives eternally, we should also live with Him (John

14:19). Though we may have to bear hardships and suffering for a little while, we are to reign with Him forever (Romans 8:18; 1 Peter 4:13). But if we deny Him and become disloyal, He cannot acknowledge us as His own (see Matthew 10:33). He is always true to His Word; therefore, it would be altogether our own fault if we should have no part in His heavenly kingdom. He has given us His Word, which we are to use as the chief weapon of our warfare (Matthew 4:4; Ephesians 6:11). We should, therefore, not permit Satan to blunt this weapon or take it from us by falsifying God's Word. Anyone who turns aside from the Gospel at any point is sure to fall into dangerous errors that harm the soul. False doctrine is like a deadly disease or cancer. It weakens and finally destroys faith. Moreover, the believer should have a firm grip on the Word of God as his or her spiritual sword. A Christian should know how to use it for combating all falsehood and ungodliness. The Word is also the believer's source of comfort and hope when the battle seems to be going against him or her. The Gospel gives the assurance that God knows and acknowledges all believers as His own, marked with a special seal for eternal life. They not only have the name of Christ on their lips but also in their hearts. For them sin is unattractive; they fight to keep it out of their lives (Galatians 5:24).

74. How does the believer remain in close communion with Jesus? What blessings does he or she enjoy because of this union?

75. Which are the two chief doctrines of Scripture? How are they to be used and applied?

In the Master's Service

Read 2 Timothy 2:20–26. Just as in a home there are utensils of different value, so also in the visible Church there are members who are precious to the Lord and those in whom He can have no delight. The hypocrites dishonor God and are not members of Christ's kingdom. Those who are acceptable to God have hearts that have been cleansed from sin and sanctified for a godly life and bring forth the fruits of faith. The believer glorifies God by works of righteousness. He or she carefully avoids what is harmful to the soul and what dishonors God. The Christian has the welfare of his or her neighbors at heart and strives with kindness and patience to instruct them in the truth and win them for Christ.

76. Why should we strive to be vessels of gold and silver in Christ's kingdom? How does a person become a "vessel for honorable use" (v. 21)?

77. Why does the apostle warn especially against youthful lusts?

In Closing

Encourage participants to begin the following activities:
- Read Matthew 24:45–51 and Luke 12:35–48. How may pastors be either those who by preaching the Gospel and the cross faithfully feed God's people the grace of Christ or those who by preaching Law and glory abuse God's people and extort false good works from them?
- In preparation for the next session, read 2 Timothy 3.

Close with prayer.

Lesson 10

The Believer's Security
in an Evil World

Why may we rely upon every statement in the Bible as absolute truth, even when it foretells what will happen in future times? We have the clearest answer to this question in our text when it makes the claim that it is the inspired Word of God. We also have a practical proof that this claim is true. The chapter that we are studying pictures conditions in the world just as they are today. The Holy Spirit showed Paul what dangers would threaten Christians as the world approached its end.

The Moral Condition of the World

Read 2 Timothy 3:1–5. The apostle had ample opportunity to become acquainted with the world of his day. Wherever he went, he met idolatry and wickedness, and it must have seemed to him that the world could never become worse than it was at that time. But as God enabled him to take a prophetic look into the distant future, he saw that the world would grow more and more evil as time went on. The closer Judgment Day approaches, the more perilous will the times be for the Church and believers. What a terrible and true picture of the world as described by the apostle and as we know it today! Paul says that it will be full of selfishness, greed, boastfulness, pride, and wickedness. People will reject God and use His name only in blasphemous speech. They will refuse to obey parents and superiors, be ungrateful for benefits received, show no respect for holy things, and not even regard their closest relatives. They will make promises without intending to keep them, ruin people's reputations for personal gain, give free reign to their sinful passions, and vent their spite on those who try to live uprightly. They will betray their neighbors and stubbornly demand to have their own way in everything. Their only purpose in life will be to enjoy the pleasures of this world. Some might even claim to be members of the Church, but their conduct will show that they are hypocrites, giving evidence that the Gospel is not at work in their hearts.

78. Why do we believe that we are living in the last days, the time near the end of the world?

79. Which sins mentioned by Paul are especially common today? Why are these a peril to Christians?

The Attitude of the World toward the Church

Read verses 6–13. Satan's chief aim is to bring the world into the Church, so that through laxity of religion and morals believers may lose their faith. He knows that his success will be greatest if he succeeds in undermining the home. Paul warns that immoral people and false teachers will carry their poisonous teachings into the houses of people who are no longer sound in the faith and will destroy their morals. People will gradually lose all understanding of what is right and wrong and close their hearts to the truth. Moreover, the devil's agents will be particularly active in trying to counteract the preaching of God's Word, just as the Egyptian sorcerers did in Moses' time. By corrupting the minds of the people, the deceivers will prevent their victims from believing the Gospel. It is remarkable what foolish things people who reject the truth will believe.

If the world fails to entice the Christian away from the truth, it has another method by which it tries to destroy him or her: persecution. Paul could not be shaken in his faith by false doctrine. Therefore, his enemies tried to crush him by persecuting him and seeking his life. Timothy himself had seen what Paul had to endure for the sake of the Gospel. In Lystra, Timothy's hometown, Paul had been stoned by a mob and dragged out of the city as dead (Acts 14:19). But God had always protected His apostle and delivered him out of all danger. Paul knew he was safe in God's hand, and he was not afraid of his enemies. He encouraged all believers to remain firm in the faith and live godly lives, even though they might have to suffer for it. What Paul says in 2 Timothy 3:12 holds true to the end of time. The world will always hate and persecute Christians.

80. What false teachers and cults have been working actively in homes and among women?

81. Why do so many people believe the ridiculous claims of false teachers and religious quacks?

82. Are Christians still persecuted today?

83. How does the world show that it hates the true believers?

84. Why is persecution a blessing to the Church?

The Source of the Christian's Power

Read verses 14–17. There is just one thing for the believer to do to keep his or her faith and not be overcome by the evil world: hold fast to the Word of God. Paul admonished Timothy to continue in the things that he had learned and been assured of by the apostle's teaching. Since his childhood, Timothy had received instruction in the

Scriptures and had become thoroughly acquainted with its teachings. This knowledge was infinitely more valuable to him than all the wisdom of the world, because it showed him the way to eternal salvation. The Scriptures led him to believe in Jesus and kept him in this faith. No one could rob him of his faith as long as it was built upon the firm foundation of God's Word. Paul emphatically states that every word of the Bible is the inspired Word of God. Therefore, it is absolutely true and infallible. Because the Christian's faith rests upon the divine authority of the sacred Scriptures, it has a tremendous power in his or her life. Paul shows how wonderfully the divinely-inspired Word serves people. One who diligently studies it and follows its teachings will derive inestimable benefits from it for faith and life and will learn how to serve God. The Bible is of greatest value because it teaches people all that they need to know about the way of salvation, shows them what things to avoid as dangerous to their souls, helps them to turn away from sin, and enables them to live holy lives. It equips people to serve God with good works. A book that is able to change the heart and life of a sinner and make him or her perfect in the eyes of God certainly must be the Word of God.

85. Who taught Timothy the Scriptures (2 Timothy 1:2, 5)?

86. How long should one continue to study the Bible? Why?

87. In what respects is the Bible different from all other books?

88. How do we know that every word in the Bible was written by divine inspiration (2 Peter 1:21; 1 Corinthians 2:13; 2 Thessalonians 2:15; John 5:39)?

89. Why should we hold firmly to the doctrine of verbal (the very words and not just the thoughts) and plenary (each and every word) inspiration?

In Closing

Encourage participants to begin the following activities:
- Read 1 Peter 1:10–12 and 2 Peter 1:16–21. Discuss the divine origin and character of the Bible as the Word of God.
- Ask participants to list ways in which the divine truthfulness of Scripture has given assurance to their faith in Jesus Christ.
- In preparation for the next session, read 2 Timothy 4.

Close with prayer.

Lesson 11

The Reward of a Godly Life

The Bible clearly teaches that no one can be saved by trying to keep God's commandments (Romans 3:28). Jesus Himself told His disciples that they could not claim any reward for their good works (Luke 17:10). Why then should a believer strive to live a godly life? Indeed, he or she should not do it for the sake of reward but to honor and please God. Nevertheless, the Lord assures us that He will graciously reward the good works produced as the fruits of our faith. Paul was certain that a crown of glory awaited him in heaven.

A Well-Spent Life

Read 2 Timothy 4:1–5. When we close our eyes in death, we do not want to feel that our life on earth was a miserable failure. It will not be so if we, like Paul and Timothy, have faithfully kept the charge that Christ has committed to us. That charge is nothing other than the Gospel, which is kept through faith alone. It is through faith that all faithfulness to His Word and love to neighbor come about. What is it that our Savior wants us to do for Him while we are waiting for His coming to take us home to heaven? Paul sums it up thus: "Preach the Word" (v. 2). Of course, the apostle addresses these words to Timothy and to all Christian pastors. But it is the responsibility of all Christians, the whole Church, to see to it that the Gospel is preached in all the world (Matthew 28:19–20; Mark 16:15). This is done through the Office of the Holy Ministry on behalf of the congregation in the name of Christ as Christian pastors preach and teach the Word of God and rightly administer the Sacraments. Each individual believer can have a part in this great work as well. Though he or she is not called to perform the work of public ministry—baptizing and teaching all things—he or she can bear witness to Christ and tell others about the Savior. Believers can support those who preach the Gospel and can be a powerful and living sermon to the world by their example. Laypeople are of greatest benefit to the Gospel when they receive the ministry of their pastors and go forth into the world and in their vocations and communities live out their faith. The world needs the Gospel, whether it wants to hear it or not. Therefore, Christians should always be at it, trying to evangelize the world. Because Satan is working so hard to keep the ungodly in his power, we Christians should work all the more faithfully as the Lord's witnesses to show people the way of salvation.

90. When may it be said that a Christian has lived a useful life?

91. Why and how should every Christian take an active part in the work of evangelism and missions?

92. Why should the nearness of Judgment Day spur us on to greater efforts in serving our fellow men with the Gospel?

The Prospect of a Heavenly Crown

Read 2 Timothy 4:6–8. Paul knew that the end of his life was at hand. But the approach of death did not cause him to fear or feel unhappy (Philippians 1:21). With calm and cheerful confidence, he could look forward to the future. He was fully prepared to die and leave this world. He had no regrets as to his past life. He knew that all his sins were forgiven and that through Christ he had become righteous before God. His past life had been a hard and long fight, but it was a good fight because he had lived and struggled for a good cause and was now about to receive the crown of victory. Paul had always fought as a loyal soldier of Jesus; like a well-trained athlete, he had run the race until he reached the goal; like a watchman, he had faithfully guarded the doctrine against corruption and error. At last his work on earth was finished. What a blessed and successful life it was! But Paul's eyes were joyfully fixed on the glorious prospect that lay before him. He was sure that he would shortly be crowned with everlasting life. God had prepared this crown for him as a gracious reward for the services he rendered to his Master. But Paul assures all believers that there is such a crown in readiness for all who love their Savior. It is not a perishable crown, but it is a heavenly crown of righteousness and perfection, which bestows upon the saint special honor and glory,

93. What does it mean to fight the good fight, finish the race, and keep the faith?

94. How is the crown described in James 1:12; Revelation 2:10; 1 Peter 5:4; 1 Corinthians 9:25? Will all the saints in heaven possess the same degree of glory (2 Corinthians 9:6; Daniel 12:3)?

Final Deliverance

Read 2 Timothy 4:9–18. The last days of Paul brought him sorrows and disappointment as far as his friends were concerned. Demas, one of his trusted helpers, had become disloyal not only to the apostle but also to Christ. Crescens, Titus, and Tychicus were unable to be with him because of duties elsewhere. Only the physician Luke was with him to cheer him. Paul was very anxious to see Timothy once more before his end, and he urged his friend to come as quickly as possible and also to bring John Mark along. He was evidently suffering discomfort in a cold dungeon and was very lonesome. Therefore, he wished to have his cloak and his books, which he had left at Troas. Paul's case had first been heard before Nero. It seems that a coppersmith by the name of Alexander had falsely accused Paul before the emperor. Some of his former friends, who could have spoken in his defense, were conspicuous by their absence. Paul prayed that God would forgive them their sins of disloyalty. As far as human help was concerned, Paul was all alone, yet he was not alone as far as God was concerned. The Lord Jesus let him know that He was at his side. He strengthened His faithful apostle and caused the first trial to result in a continuance of his case. Even though he knew that he would finally die a martyr's death, Paul realized that it would only mean final deliverance from all evil. Soon he would be in heaven with his Savior. Thus, he glorified God to the very end of his life. With some personal greetings and a final blessing upon Timothy, Paul laid aside his pen for the last time.

95. In what respect is Demas a lesson of warning?

96. What are the final impressions the Bible leaves of Timothy? Mark? Paul?

97. What comfort does verse 18 contain? Of which petition does this verse remind us?

In Closing

Encourage participants to begin the following activities:
- Compare the spirit of our Lord in His passion and death (Matthew 26–27; Mark 14–15; Luke 22–23; John 18–19) with Paul's in his final days (2 Timothy 4:6–18).
- In preparation for the next session, read Titus 1:1–2:10.

Close with prayer.

Lesson 12

A Summary of the Christian Life

The short epistle to Titus contains advice to a young pastor, which is in most points practically the same as what Paul had already written to Timothy. Both helpers of the apostle were stationed in difficult fields and needed his guidance and encouragement. The similarity of these epistles does not make any of them superfluous to us. The study of this shorter letter gives us a splendid opportunity to review and fix more firmly in our minds the lessons that we have studied in the epistles to Timothy.

A Blameless Ministry

Read Titus 1:1–9. This letter has a much longer introduction than the epistles to Timothy. Paul wanted the people in Crete to acknowledge his authority as an apostle of Christ who had been commissioned to preach the Gospel to them. His message was the divine truth, which was to lead them to faith and godliness and fill them with the hope of eternal life. Since Paul had been able to stay with them only a short time, they were to regard Titus as his representative, whose chief duty was to help them obtain faithful pastors and provide them with an orderly form of church government.

In verses 6–9, Paul again specifies the qualifications that a pastor should have. Compare this list with 1 Timothy 3. In regard to his conduct, a pastor should be above reproach. He should have a good reputation and possess all Christian virtues in a high degree. He should above all hold firmly to the pure doctrine and be able to defend it against false teachers.

98. How does Paul in each of the Pastoral Epistles set forth his official position?

99. Why does Paul lay so much stress on sound doctrine?

A Pure Church

Read Titus 1:10–16. Paul warned Titus against false teachers and ungodly people, just as he had warned Timothy. It seems that Jewish errorists were trying to turn the Cretans against the Gospel. By means of their false doctrines, they sought to enrich themselves and exercise control over the people. Crete was a fertile field for deceivers and religious quacks. Paul knew from experience that the Cretans could not be trusted and that they were unstable and lazy people. Their own poets had complained about these evil traits. Paul urged Titus to preach the Law to the unruly and wicked, but if they repented, he should, by means of the Gospel, teach them the way of godliness.

100. What attitude should the Church take toward religious deceivers? What harm is done by them?

Christian Character and Conduct

Read Titus 2:1–10. Paul shows Titus how he is to apply the sound doctrine of the Word to individual church members. Regardless of their age or sex, people should constantly be on their guard against particular temptations and sins and should strive to live exemplary lives. Titus was to be to his flock a "model of good works" (v. 7). As a pastor, it was his duty to teach by word and example that the Christians should keep the Gospel pure and live sincerely according to it, so that, if anyone would speak evil of them, he would not be able to prove his charges. Finally, Titus was to admonish the Christian slaves to be obedient and faithful to their masters and to warn them not to become guilty of petty stealing (pilfering), a sin that has been frequently committed by slaves and servants. By rendering faithful service, they would help bring the Christian religion into favor with their masters and prove that the Gospel is a great power for good in the world.

101. What Christian qualities should be strongly developed in older Christians?

102. What are our obligations toward our supervisors and employers (1 Timothy 6:1–2)?

In Closing

Encourage participants to begin the following activities:
- Discuss what motivates professing Christians to turn away from the truth.
- Recount briefly how a mature Christian influenced participants' lives.
- In preparation for the next session, read Titus 2:11–3:15.

Close with prayer.

Lesson 13

A Summary of the Christian Faith

The second part of Paul's Letter to Titus contains a beautiful summary of the Gospel, which the ancient Church selected as the Epistle lesson for the Christmas Festival. In the third chapter, we meet with that well-known passage that Luther quotes in his catechism to illustrate the power of Holy Baptism. In our final lesson on the Pastoral Epistles, the apostle paints a magnificent picture of the intimate relationship between a believer and his or her God.

Salvation by Grace

Read Titus 2:11–15. In a stirring hymn of praise, Paul glorifies God for having, in His infinite grace, prepared salvation for all people. Paul also shows what a great change the Gospel produces in our hearts and lives. God does not want us, upon whom He has bestowed forgiveness and eternal life, to continue in sin. Instead, He desires that we should serve Him in holiness and godliness as people who hope to be with Him forever in heaven. Jesus died for us in order that He might take away our sins and make us to be God's people who delight in serving God with their good works (1 Peter 2:9). Titus was to teach these important truths regarding our redemption and sanctification. As a called minister of God, he was to preach both the Law and the Gospel and apply them to the needs of his hearers. The people were to show him proper respect and receive his message as the Word of God.

103. What effect should the Gospel have on our lives?

104. How are we to regard those who preach the Gospel (Luke 10:16; 1 Timothy 4:12; 5:17)?

The New Birth

Read Titus 3:1–7. Christians are to show by their attitude toward their neighbor that they are the children of God. They should render faithful obedience to their government and be willing to do anything whereby others will be benefited. Malicious gossiping, quarreling, and other objectionable traits should not be found among Christians. They are able to walk the way of righteousness, because they have been born again spiritually unto a life of faith and godliness (John 3:5). By means of Holy Baptism, the Holy Spirit has cleansed us from our sins and created in us the new life of faith, which lays hold to the salvation of Jesus. Because Baptism works this change in us and makes us children of God, it is called the "washing of regeneration and renewal of the Holy Spirit" (Titus 3:5). It bestows upon us all the blessings of Christ's redemption and makes us heirs of eternal life.

105. Why may Christians not boast that before their conversion they were by nature better than unbelievers (v. 3; Ephesians 2:1–2)?

106. Why must we be born again before we can be children of God (John 3:3–5)?

107. How does Paul prove that our redemption and sanctification are entirely and solely the work of God?

108. How does he prove that Baptism is a means of grace and has the power to work faith in one's spiritual life (Titus 3:5)? Is this an argument for or against infant Baptism?

109. How does Luther explain the value and power of Baptism in his catechism?

The Fruits of Faith

Read Titus 3:8–15. The Gospel, which is absolutely trustworthy because it is God's Word, is to be preached constantly to believers so that they may remain in fellowship with God and become more and more like Him in holiness. One who truly lives a Christian life will be able to render the most profitable service to one's neighbor. A strong faith is our best safeguard against all religious errors and delusions of people. The Church should not tolerate false teachers (heretics) in its midst. If these stubbornly persist in their antibiblical views, they should be put out of the Church as people who have condemned themselves by deliberately rejecting the truth.

Before closing his letter, Paul urged Titus to join him at Nicopolis, where he intended to spend the winter. Meanwhile, either Artemas or Tychicus would take Titus's place on Crete. Titus was asked to assist Zenas and Apollos on their way to some mission field to which Paul was sending them. By giving these missionaries all possible support, the Christians on the isle of Crete would be making good use of their opportunity to give evidence of their faith, and they would receive valuable training in Christian giving (v. 14). The epistle closes with a cordial greeting to Titus and all believers.

110. Why should we be constantly reminded of our redemption, justification, and heavenly heritage (v. 8; 2:14; 2 Timothy 2:21; 3:17)?

111. What should be a Christian's attitude toward false teachers (v. 10; Romans 16:17)?

112. Why should we do all we can for our missionaries?

In Closing

Encourage participants to begin the following activities:
* Read Matthew 28:19, 20; Mark 16:15, 16; Luke 24:45–49; John 20:21–23. Discuss how the work of the pastoral office carries out and fulfills the Gospel ministry mandated by Jesus.
* Ask class members what their study of the Pastoral Epistles has taught them and how their faith has been edified.

Close with prayer.

Leader Notes

This guide is provided as a safety net, a place to turn for help in answering questions and for enriching discussion. It will not answer every question raised in your class. Please read it along with the questions before class. Consult it in class only after exploring the Bible references and discussing what they teach. Please note the different abilities of your class members. Some will easily find the Bible passages listed in this study; others will struggle. To make participation easier, team up members of the class. For example, if a question asks you to look up several passages, assign one passage to one group, the second to another, and so on. Divide the work! Let participants present the answers they discover.

Preparing to Teach 1 and 2 Timothy and Titus

To prepare to lead this study, read through the Books of 1 and 2 Timothy and Titus. You might review the introduction to these books in the *Concordia Self-Study Bible* or a Bible handbook. A map of the Roman world (especially the lands surrounding the Mediterranean Sea) and a map showing Paul's travels would also help.

If you have the opportunity, you will find it helpful to make use of other biblical reference works in the course of your study. These commentaries can be very helpful: Victor A. Bartling, H. Armin Moellering, *1 Timothy, 2 Timothy, Titus, Philemon*, Concordia Commentary (St. Louis: Concordia Publishing House, 1970); Armin W. Schuetze, *1 and 2 Timothy, Titus*, People's Bible Commentary (St. Louis: Concordia Publishing House, 1995); Donald Guthrie, *The Pastoral Epistles: An Introduction and Commentary*, Tyndale New Testament Commentaries (Grand Rapids: Wm. B. Eerdmans Publishing Company, 1990). Although it is not strictly a commentary, the sections on 1 and 2 Timothy and Titus in *The Word Becoming Flesh* by Horace Hummel (St. Louis: Concordia Publishing House, 1979) also contains valuable material for the proper interpretation of this biblical book.

Group Bible Study

Group Bible study means mutual learning from one another under the guidance of a leader. The Bible is an inexhaustible resource. No one person can discover all it has to offer. In any class, many eyes see many things, things that can be applied to many life situations. The leader should resist the temptation to give the answers and so act as an authority. This teaching approach stifles participation by individual members and can actually hamper learning. As a general rule, don't give interpretation. Instead, develop interpreters. In other words, don't explain what the learners can discover by themselves. This is not to say that the leader shouldn't share insights and information gained by his or her class members during the lesson, engage them in meaningful sharing and discussion, or lead them to a summary of the lesson at the close.

Have a chalkboard and chalk or newsprint and marker available to emphasize significant points of the lesson. Rephrase your inquiries or the inquiries of participants as questions, problems, or issues. This provokes thought. Keep discussion to the point. List the answers given on the chalkboard or newsprint. Then determine the most vital points made in the discussion. Ask additional questions to fill gaps.

The aim of every Bible study is to help people grow spiritually, not merely in biblical and theological knowledge, but in Christian thinking and living. This means growth in Christian attitudes, insights, and skills for Christian living. The focus of this course must be the Church and the world of our day. The guiding question will be this: What does the Lord teach us for life today through 1 and 2 Timothy and Titus?

Teaching the New Testament

Teaching a New Testament Letter that was originally written for and read to first-century Christians can become merely ancient history if not applied to life in our times. Leaders need to understand the time and culture in which the Letter was written. They need to understand the historical situation of the Early Church and the social and cultural setting in which that Church existed. Such background information can clarify the original purpose and meaning of the Letter and shed light on its meaning for Christians today. For this reason, Bible commentaries and other reference works are indispensable when it comes to leading Bible studies.

Teaching the Bible can easily degenerate into mere moralizing, in which do-goodism or rules become substitutes for the Gospel, and sanctification is confused with justification. Actually, justified sinners are moved not by Law but by God's grace to a totally new life. Their faith is always at work for Christ in every context of life. Meaningful, personal Christianity consists of a loving trust in God that is evidenced in love for others. Having experienced God's free grace and forgiveness, Christians daily work in their world to reflect the will of God for people in every area of human endeavor.

Christian leaders are Gospel-oriented, not Law-oriented; they distinguish between the two. Both Law and Gospel are necessary. The Gospel will mean nothing unless we first have been crushed by the Law and see our sinfulness. There is no genuine Christianity if faith is not followed by lives pleasing to God. In fact, genuine faith is inseparable from life. The Gospel alone gives us the new heart that causes us to love God and our neighbor.

Pace Your Teaching

The lessons in this course of study are designed for a study session of at least an hour in length. If it is the desire and intent of the class to complete an entire lesson each session, it will be necessary for you to summarize the content of certain answers or biblical references in order to preserve time. Asking various class members to look up different Bible passages and to read them aloud to the rest of the class will save time over having every class member look up each reference.

Also, you may not want to cover every question in each lesson. This may lead to undue haste and frustration. Be selective. Pace your teaching. Spend no more than five to ten minutes opening the lesson. During the lesson, get the sweep of meaning. Occasionally stop to help the class gain understanding of a word or concept. Allow approximately five minutes for closing and announcements.

Should your group have more than a one-hour class period, you can take it more leisurely, but do not allow any lesson to drag and become tiresome. Keep it moving. Keep it alive. Keep it meaningful. Eliminate some questions and restrict yourself to those questions most meaningful to the members of the class. If most members study the text at home, they can report their findings, and the time gained can be applied to relating the lesson to life.

Good Preparation

Good preparation by the leader usually affects the pleasure and satisfaction the class will experience.

Suggestions to the Leader for Using the Study Guide

This set of lessons is designed to aid Bible study, that is, to aid a consideration of the written Word of God, with discussion and personal application growing out of the text at hand.

The typical lesson is divided into these sections:
1. Theme Verse
2. Objectives
3. Questions and Answers
4. Closing

The theme verse and objectives give you, the leader, assistance in arousing the interest of the group in the concepts of the lesson. Focus on stimulating minds. Do not linger too long over the introductory remarks.

The questions and answers provide the real spadework necessary for Bible study. Here the class digs, uncovers, and discovers; it gets the facts and observes them. Comments from the leader are needed only to the extent that they help the group understand the text. The questions in this guide, corresponding to sections within the text, are intended to help the participants discover the meaning of the text.

Having determined what the text says, the class is ready to apply the message. Having heard, read, marked, and learned the Word of God, they can proceed to digest it inwardly through discussion, evaluation, and application. This is done, as this guide suggests, by taking the truths found in Scripture and applying them to the world and Christianity in general, and then to one's personal Christian life. Class time may not permit discussion of all questions and topics. In preparation, you may need to select one or two and focus on them. Close the session by reviewing one important truth from the lesson.

Remember, the Word of God is sacred, but this study guide is not. The notes in this section offer only guidelines and suggestions. Do not hesitate to alter the guidelines or substitute others to meet your needs and the needs of the participants. Adapt your teaching plan to your class and your class period.

Good teaching directs the learner to discover for himself or herself. For the teacher, this means directing the learner but not giving the learner answers. Directing understanding takes preparation. Choose the verses that should be looked up in Scripture ahead of time. What discussion questions will you ask? at what points? Write them in the margin of your study guide. Involve class members, but give them clear directions. What practical actions might you propose for the week following the lesson? Which of the items do you consider most important for your class?

Consider how you can best use your teaching period. Do you have forty-five minutes, an hour, or an hour and a half? If time is short, what should you cut? Learn to become a wise steward of class time.

Plan a brief opening devotion using members of the class. At the end, be sure to take time to summarize the lesson or have a class member do it.

Remember to pray frequently for yourself and your class. May God the Holy Spirit bless your study and your leading of others into the comforting truths of God's Christ-centered Word.

Lesson 1

The Pastoral Epistles

Theme verse: *To Timothy, my true child in the faith: Grace, mercy, and peace, from God the Father and Christ Jesus our Lord.*

1 Timothy 1:2

Objectives

By the power of the Holy Spirit working through God's Word, we will:
- understand under what circumstances and for what purposes the Pastoral Epistles were written;
- become familiar with the general plan and scope of these letters;
- gain a basic appreciation for the work of the ministry.

1. Timothy may have been converted under Paul's ministry at Lystra during his first missionary tour (Acts 14:5–23). He is brought to Paul's attention by the churches in Lystra and Iconium who speak well of him, and Paul takes Timothy along with him and Silas. He continues with Paul and Silas to Philippi (where a church is founded and Paul and Silas are imprisoned), Thessalonica, and Berea (where he stayed with Silas after Paul was conducted out of the city to Athens).

At some point during this time, he is sent to Thessalonica to conduct pastoral ministry in order to preserve the church there (1 Thessalonians 3:1–5). He and Silas join Paul in Corinth (Acts 18:5) and apparently accompany Paul for the rest of the tour.

Timothy is with Paul on the third missionary tour (AD 53–57), leaving from Antioch and heading immediately for southern Galatia and westward to Phrygia "strengthening all the disciples" (Acts 18:23). They return to Ephesus where Paul spent no less than two years and enjoyed a powerful ministry (Acts 19:10, 20). At some point, Timothy and Erastus are dispatched to Macedonia (Acts 19:22) and then proceed southward to Corinth (1 Corinthians 4:17; 16:10, 11; 2 Timothy 4:20).

Paul leaves Ephesus, travels through Macedonia, and arrives in Greece where Timothy and Erastus are ministering, and spends three months there (Acts 20:2). Immediately, Paul decides to travel back to Syria from Philippi instead of the nearby port of Cenchrea, because he had learned of a plot on his life by the Jews (Acts 20:3). He and an entourage, including Timothy, retrace their steps back up through Macedonia to Philippi (Acts 20:2–4).

Timothy and the entourage go to Troas, where Paul catches up five days later to stay with them for a week (Acts 20:6). Timothy apparently accompanies Paul for the remainder of the third tour (Acts 20:13–21).

From Rome, Paul sends Timothy to the Philippian Church. Later, after his release, Paul embarks on a fourth missionary tour, visiting Ephesus, where he assigns Timothy pastoral work.

Paul summons Timothy to Rome, where the apostle is languishing in a dungeon. He is to come soon and on his way pick up John Mark and retrieve Paul's cloak as well as scrolls and parchments. Later, Timothy himself suffers imprisonment (Hebrews 13:23).

2. Paul shows his personal affection for Timothy, calling him his "true child" and "beloved child." These terms are also important in recognizing Timothy's authority and legitimacy as the one called and ordained to carry on the Gospel ministry there at Ephesus.

3. In Philippians, Paul expresses confidence that through the prayers of fellow Christians his release will occur. However, in 2 Timothy, he says that his departure has come. It is by God's grace alone that in either case Paul and all Christians are well-prepared.

4. Paul desired to see Timothy personally not only out of need but because Timothy's presence would bring him joy. When we are isolated and alone, especially where we are contending for the faith, those who along with us faithfully confess pure doctrine minister to us.

5. It is clear that Titus was a vital part of Paul's ministry in Greece and Asia Minor. He is a trusted brother and esteemed minister of the Gospel. He shared Paul's own pastoral work and spirit in ministering to the difficult church in Corinth. Titus was charged with receiving a collection from the Corinthians and showed pastoral sensitivity in dealing with them in the face of a disciplinary matter.

6. Titus is called "my true child in a common faith" (Titus 1:4). As with Timothy, Paul is reminding all who would question Titus's authority or legitimacy that Paul himself has appointed this man and he enjoys the apostle's full approval. The words "in a common faith" affirm that Titus's doctrine is that which is revealed in the Gospel and therefore known and believed by all true Christians and not like that of false teachers, which is private doctrine that only specially anointed teachers may know.

The work assigned to Titus is the completion of the church-planting work on Crete. This is seen primarily in the ordaining of men to the pastoral office. This is because Christ has instituted the pastoral office as the agent through which the Church's ministry is to be carried out. It is Christ's love-gift to the body to perform the work of service to His saints and build up the body of Christ through the Gospel (Ephesians 4:11–12). Whatever else a church may do or seek, its first priority should be to insure the presence and service of a pastor.

7. Citing a Cretan poet, he says they are "liars, evil beasts, lazy gluttons" (Titus 1:12). Is this merely a case of name calling? (Remember, the Holy Spirit inspired these words, and therefore they are God's.) No, this is really just a description of the Old Adam in all of us and how it manifested itself in a particular culture. What sins are prevalent in your community or culture that interfere with hearing and believing the Gospel and pure doctrine?

8. First, this teaches us what we are to expect from the Church and the ministry of the Gospel. Christians often have unbiblical expectations that prevent them from appreciating and receiving the true gifts of Christ. The Augsburg Confession says that through the public ministry we are granted "not only bodily, but also eternal things: eternal righteousness, the Holy Spirit, and eternal life" (AC XXVIII 8). Second, it helps believers to better assist and pray for their pastors. Third, the spiritual truths spoken here apply in many respects to all believers as they touch upon "all who desire to live a godly life in Christ Jesus" (2 Timothy 3:12).

Lesson 2

The Firm Foundation of Our Faith

Theme verse: *This charge I entrust to you, Timothy, my child, in accordance with the prophecies previously made about you, that by them you may wage the good warfare.*

1 Timothy 1:18

Objectives

By the power of the Holy Spirit working through God's Word, we will:

- understand how important sound doctrine is both for coming to faith and for remaining in the faith;
- recognize the nature of false doctrine and its destructive effects;
- learn how the pastoral office serves to keep our faith sound.

Timothy's chief problem in Ephesus was how to deal with certain persons who were confusing the Christians by their peculiar views and false doctrines. Paul wanted these disturbers of the faith to be stopped. Timothy was to defend the truth against them and to warn them not to teach contrary to the Gospel.

9. In Ephesus, false teachers speculated about matters that had no spiritual value and distracted the attention of the people from the important teachings of God's Word. Fanciful Jewish fictional tales and Old Testament lists of ancestors were made the basis of their discussions, probably of their sermons in church services. They played with the Word of God instead of interpreting it correctly and applying it to the needs of the people. They turned people's minds away from

the Gospel. Today, for example, one can find teaching on life skills, personal finances, or so-called personality inventories and personality types. Others who want to be conservative and Scriptural harp constantly on the Law and teach works righteousness and morality as the essence of Christianity.

10. Those in Ephesus boasted of the Law, but they showed that they had no understanding of the right use of the Law. They prescribed the Law as a means of righteousness and gaining favor with God, when in fact the Law is "not laid down for the just but for the lawless and disobedient" (1 Timothy 1:9). Such methods do not promote growth in the knowledge of God's Word but lead people away from the Gospel. Paul warns all Christians not to listen to such teachers.

11. Paul does not say the Law is of no concern to the believer. He only argues against its wrong use. What was wrong with the false teachers in Ephesus was that they preached the Law in a manner that would overthrow faith. The Law is also the Word of God, and therefore it is good, but it is not able to make a sinner righteous, that is, convert, regenerate, and sanctify him or her. The Law is for the wicked to lead them to a knowledge of their sins. It serves the sinner in three ways: first, as a curb; second, as a mirror; and third, as a rule or guide for the Christian life. Here, however, Paul does not discuss the third use.

12. Paul illustrates how the Gospel works faith and regenerates the sinner by his own example. All his ability as a Christian and as a preacher of the Gospel he derived from the mercy that Christ had shown to him. It was not by the works of the Law but by the grace of God that he was justified.

13. Salvation is God's free gift of grace of which no one is worthy, not even the great apostle Paul. He had been a strict Pharisee and showed great zeal for the Law, but in spite of that he had been a great sinner. He could never forget that he had persecuted the Church (Acts 9:4, 5; 22:4, 7; 26:11). He had blasphemed the holy name of Jesus and had done much harm to God's people.

14. The unbounded grace of God, which Paul experienced, was henceforth the great theme of his thoughts and speech. Paul has four other faithful sayings in the Pastoral Epistles: 1 Timothy 3:1; 4:9; 2 Timothy 2:11; Titus 3:8. In a very emphatic manner, he states that the Gospel is reliable and trustworthy.

15. The apostle wanted his young friend to remain in this faith and grow stronger therein. Timothy is to fight all false teachers and error with the Word of God. Paul refers to the teachings of the prophets and apostles that Timothy had pledged to preach when he was ordained to be a pastor (1 Timothy 4:14). He was well fortified and equipped for fighting against sin and error.

16. As long as a Christian remains in faith, he or she will have a good conscience before God. One cannot keep his or her faith and enjoy the peace of God in one's heart while playing fast and loose with the Word of God. Such people will become shipwrecked in the faith. Paul mentions two teachers who had this sad experience.

17. How many fall away from Christ during the years after their confirmation because they do not grow stronger in the knowledge of the sound doctrines of Scripture! Matthew 7:24 says that our faith must rest on the firm foundation of God's Word, or Satan will overthrow it.

18. Teaching false doctrine is a form of blasphemy, because it dishonors God. Satan rules over such people. The act of discipline should serve to bring offenders to repentance. No congregation should tolerate such persons in its midst.

Lesson 3

The Christian in the House of God

Theme verse: *This is good, and it is pleasing in the sight of God our Savior, who desires all people to be saved and to come to the knowledge of the truth.*

1 Timothy 2:3, 4

Objectives

By the power of the Holy Spirit working through God's Word, we will:
- understand that we should faithfully attend church services and conduct ourselves in a manner befitting the house of God;
- recognize that preaching and prayer are central to Christian worship;
- understand the proper roles of men and women in public worship.

If some prominent person should invite you to visit him or her at home, how would you conduct yourself in his or her presence? Would you not regard that as a great honor, act your very best, and try to derive as much benefit from your visit as possible? Some people seem to forget that when they are in church they are in the house and presence of God. They do not come to talk to God and hear the Lord speak to them. They regard the church as any ordinary place, where they think they can have a good time and do as they please. Not only do such people annoy others who come to worship, but they also give grave offense by their conduct and bring upon themselves judgment instead of blessing because they despise God's gifts. Let us consider how we should behave in the Lord's sanctuary.

19. Our Lord stresses the necessity of praying "in My name." This means that we present our prayers and our selves to God on the basis of Christ's mediation as our High Priest and Savior, believing that for His sake alone God will certainly hear and answer our prayers. When we take up His name in prayer, we are graciously invited by God to believe and not doubt that Jesus' name grants to us complete and eternal favor with God even though we are sinners and deserve nothing but His wrath. (Note that in the context of 1 Timothy 2, this means that we should invoke Jesus' name to ask God's mercies upon everybody, especially since He is the Savior of all people.)

20. In verse 8, Paul states several conditions of true prayer. Lifting up of hands was the Jewish prayer custom, which expressed the fact that all blessings must come from God. They stood with empty palms turned to heaven, signifying that they wished these hands to be filled. The important thing, however, is that the heart is right with God. "Without anger" (v. 8) implies that we have right feelings toward our neighbor. An angry person cannot pray. This violates the fifth petition in which we forgive others (see Matthew 5:22; 6:14–15).

21. Unbelief prevents God from answering our prayers because it holds His word of promise to be untrue and unreliable. Such prayers are not spiritual but carnal and therefore those that God does not hear.

22. Faith is created by hearing the Gospel. "So faith comes from hearing, and hearing through the word of Christ" (Romans 10:17). The preached Word is the chief means of grace, and by it God's grace is both offered and conferred upon people.

23. Salvation is received only through faith and is given by means of the Gospel, which presents Christ as the mediator between God and mankind. A mediator is one who makes peace between two parties. Christ's atonement came in between God and the sinful world. He settled our account with God and reconciled us to God by paying the ransom for our sins. We may be assured of salvation since Christ's mediation promises us unconditional and eternal acceptance by God.

24. It is God's will that the Gospel be preached to all people. Since God wants all people to be saved, we should also have the same desire and seek its realization by means of our prayers and missionary efforts.

25. Paul is still speaking of public worship, but he is now referring in particular to women. The apostle first speaks of women's dress and outward appearance in public worship. He does not forbid all adornment, nor does he encourage slovenliness. The chief thing is that decency and modesty be observed. Anything that attracts attention and is apt to disturb the worshiper should be avoided. A Christian life of good works is the adornment that pleases God. Second, Paul sets forth women's relation to the congregation and the ministry. What he says here holds for all time (1 Corinthians 14:34–35). He is stating a divine principle that cannot be altered by human beings. Women are to be silent in the public services of the Church. This means they are to be recipients of ministerial service and not those who perform it. They are not to assist in conducting the church services, not to serve in the ministry, and are not to lead public prayer (Ephesians 5:22; Colossians 3:18; 1 Peter 3:1).

26. The reason for this is found in the original order of woman's relation to man in which she is created subordinate to the man but in no way inferior (Genesis 2:18–23; 1 Corinthians 11:8–9). God does not want women to assume leadership over men. The second reason for this divine arrangement is that woman was the first to fall into sin. Eve caused Adam to sin by acting as his leader. She thereby deserted her divinely-assigned position and demonstrated her inability to lead her husband. Christianity does not alter the position and sphere assigned to the sexes at the time of creation.

27. Nevertheless, the Christian religion has restored woman to her position of honor as man's companion and helpmate. Women may teach children and other women (2 Timothy 1:5; 3:15; Titus 2:3–4), but they may not publicly teach men. There is no place for female pastors in the Christian Church. Women should not hold any position in the Church in which she would be the head over a man or over men. If she is married, a woman's proper and primary sphere of life is in the home, which means in relation to her husband and children. She is not in the least curtailed as far as her spiritual life is concerned (Galatians 3:28). By faithfully performing the duties assigned to them and rearing their children in the fear of God, Christian women give evidence of their faith. In heaven, God will graciously reward them for their good works.

Lesson 4

Serving the Lord in Church

Theme verse: *If I delay, you may know how one ought to behave in the household of God, which is the church of the living God, a pillar and buttress of truth.*

1 Timothy 3:15

Objectives

By the power of the Holy Spirit working through God's Word, we will:

- understand the qualifications and duties of pastors and church workers in general;
- be encouraged to use our talents as much as possible in service to the Church;
- appreciate the importance of Gospel-centered ministry and worship.

Some churches permit any person in the services to get up and preach if he desires to do so. Today the work of public ministry—the ministry of Word and Sacrament and the leading of public worship services—is often done by unordained and untrained men and even women. The Scriptures, however, do not give everyone the right to preach and serve as a pastor. The Augsburg Confession states that "no one should publicly teach in the Church, or administer the Sacraments, without a rightly ordered call" (AC XIV).

Why do our churches devote so much effort and expense to obtaining a pastor, and why do the church members make careful inquiry before they call a man? Because God's Word reveals how important it is that such a man have the proper qualifications.

28. In the New Testament the word *overseer* refers to the same office that is also called "pastor," which means "shepherd." The word *elder* has the same meaning (1 Timothy 5:17). There were various titles for the same office, no difference in rank being recognized until the second century. The ministry is a divine institution. For this reason and also because it ministers to the welfare of souls, it is a high and exalted office. The Church is to exercise proper care so that only such persons will be made pastors as meet the divinely-appointed requirements.

"Above reproach" means of good reputation, so that no one can prove a charge against him. "The husband of one wife" indicates not that he must be married, but if he is, he must be true to his wife, not guilty of sexual laxity. "Self-controlled" is being temperate in the use of all things, watchful over his conduct. "Sober-minded" denotes sound judgment. "Respectable" means he is orderly in mind and habits. "Hospitable" shows he is ready to give shelter to poor brothers and believers made homeless by persecution or misfortune (Romans 12:13; Hebrews 13:2; 1 Peter 4:9). "Able to teach" is a distinct requirement for pastors (see 1 Timothy 5:17; 2 Timothy 2:2; 3:14; 1 Corinthians 12:29). This is not the natural gift of teaching but the spiritual gift of teaching. It is the ability to explain clearly the mysteries of the Gospel. The blessing of the Holy Spirit working through the Word is alone what makes the pastor effective in his teaching ministry and not the use of worldly techniques. The pastor is *the* public teacher in the Church. Other verses contain negative qualities, with the one exception of being "gentle." Drunkards, the violent, and lovers of money bring discredit upon the ministry. "Violent" means being ready to resort to violence or quick with his fists. "Quarrelsome" means a pugnacious person who is always ready to squabble and fight. A pastor should be gentle, fair, yielding. He should be able to function well as the head of his own home and do all he can to rear a Christian family. A "novice" is a person who has just recently become a Christian, one who lacks experience and whose strength of character and faith have not yet been tested. Such a person might become conceited because of the trust put in him and in his pride become a prey of the devil.

29. The primary duty of the pastoral office is the proclamation of the Gospel. Consequently, pastors are to spend their time immersed in the study and contemplation of the Word of God and feeding it to God's people regularly through preaching and teaching, along with the

right administration of the Sacraments. They must demonstrate their competence in handling the Word of God by rightly and properly dividing Law and Gospel and by refuting false teachers. God's Word promises the pastor that by carefully maintaining a devout life of faith in Christ and pure doctrine, both he and his hearers will be saved (1 Timothy 4:16).

30. The New Testament has only one standard of morals for both clergy and laity, but it is a well-known fact that moral faults and weaknesses are more readily tolerated in church members than in their pastors. The reasons for making this distinction are quite evident. Members look up to their pastors as leaders and patterns. Pastors are expected to be examples to the flock (Philippians 3:17; 2 Thessalonians 3:9; 1 Peter 5:3).

31. The congregation owes the pastor recognition of his divine call to minister to them the Gospel in the stead and by the command of Christ. They must not consider or treat him as a hireling but as Christ's ambassador and gift to them to perform sacred ministry through Word and Sacrament. Consequently, the congregation must submit to the pastor's ministry through the glad, regular, and believing reception of God's grace that he ministers to them through the means of grace. They are to love and respect him for his office's sake. And finally, they should see to his material and earthly needs through an adequate salary and compensation.

32. Read Acts 6:1–6. Here the apostle gives the qualifications for deacons and deaconesses (or "wives" as the ESV translates the word), which in general apply to all church workers. The word *deacon* means a servant. This office was established in the Early Church (Acts 6). The deacons had charge of visiting the sick and distributing the funds of charity. Today the deacons, or elders, assist in keeping order in the public services, help the pastor admonish people, and maintain harmony in the congregation. In the course of time, numerous congregational and synodical offices have been added (e.g., church council, treasurer, secretary, Sunday School teachers and officers, etc.). Laypeople elected to do church work should have the proper qualifications and should be sound in all matters pertaining to their faith and Christian life. They should be dignified, meaning respectable, of serious bearing, and also not double-tongued, saying one thing to this person and the very opposite to another. They should be sincere in speech, refrain from gossiping, be temperate in eating and drinking,

and avoid the appearance of seeking personal gain. "To hold the mystery of the faith with a clear conscience" (1 Timothy 3:9) means they unreservedly and unhypocritically subscribe in faith to the Gospel. Verse 11 in some translations refers to the wives of deacons, but in others to female laborers in the congregations or deaconesses. Their duty was to nurse the sick, find shelter for travelers, and distribute alms to the poor. Both women and men who do church work must guard especially against sins of the tongue (i.e., gossip). Church workers should be faithful and trustworthy in all respects so that people have confidence in them. Lay workers must also be sexually pure (v. 12), and their home life should be above reproach. If they serve faithfully, they will be respected and honored by their fellow Christians. Since they are to serve others, their qualifications must be such as will ensure true service.

33. Every Christian represents Christ and is called to live a life of faithful devotion to Him. Both in the home and in public, our conduct bears witness to the Gospel in one way or another. A consistent life of faith in Christ and love to one's neighbor—that is, every and any other human being—furnishes a compelling witness to others of Christ.

34. All Christians should be keenly aware that in church they are in the very house of the living God. There ministers serve, and the people together worship in the presence of God who sees everything that goes on in the hearts and lives of His people. Keeping that in mind, they will refrain from pride, selfishness, quarreling, gossiping, and other evils that sometimes disturb the peace of a congregation. The Church is "a pillar and buttress of truth" (v. 15). From the Church, the truth shines out into the world and draws men to Christ.

35. The substance of the Gospel message is stated in verse 16. Paul may here be quoting a Christian hymn or psalm. Note the beautiful rhythm of the words and lines. Christ is the subject of all Christian preaching, which centers on His incarnation, redemption, and exaltation. This is the Gospel, because it shows to us the work Christ has performed for our salvation. All heavenly gifts and grace, and faith itself, come from this Gospel and to substitute for it stories, self-help plans of personal holiness, or church programs, however well-intended, is to lose all such precious blessings.

Lesson 5

Godliness in Everyday Life

Theme verse: *If you put these things before the brothers, you will be a good servant of Christ Jesus, being trained in the words of the faith and of the good doctrine that you have followed.*

1 Timothy 4:6

Objectives

By the power of the Holy Spirit working through God's Word, we will:

- understand the value of godliness;
- be encouraged to apply the teachings of God's Word to our daily lives;
- recognize the necessity and centrality of the pastoral office to the life and ministry of the Church.

Often the greatest harm is done to the Church not by its enemies but by its own members who live contrary to the Gospel. In our last session, we saw what God expects of pastors and leaders in the Church. Today we learn how vital the pastoral office is to the life and ministry of the Church. The Pastoral Epistles refer to the Christian life and Gospel ministry as "godliness." This is nothing else than faith in Christ and the life of love freely lived under the grace given us through Him. It stands opposite to false godliness, which stresses human works and self-righteousness.

36. Everybody tries to get as much out of life as he or she possibly can. But there is a wrong as well as a right way to go about this. Paul warns us not to follow the advice of people who have set up altogether wrong aims of life. If we listen to them, we shall lose not only the really good things in life but finally life itself. In our text, the

apostle paints a true picture of the great spiritual dangers that confront us today. He was not merely imagining what might happen in days to come. He had received a clear and direct revelation from the Holy Spirit (2 Thessalonians 2:1–11; 2 Timothy 3:1–8; 2 Peter 3:2). This prophecy has come true, as we can easily see. Paul mentions two satanic errors that have played much havoc in the Church: required abstinence from marriage and from certain foods. Even in the Early Church, there were sects that held that marriage is unclean and sinful and prescribed rules for fasting as necessary for salvation. These errors were particularly developed in the papacy. For example, clergy are not permitted to marry, and at one time meat was not to be eaten on Friday. There is also the practice of asceticism—extreme self-denial and harsh treatment of the body to gain spiritual grace—and the monastic life of monks and nuns that is taken up with the belief that it is spiritually superior to ordinary life (Colossians 2:16; 1 Corinthians 10:31).

Today many teach that upon meeting certain conditions of devotedness, surrender, or obedience, Christians may secure from God certain blessings. Greater levels of grace and spiritual illumination are said to be available if one will follow a certain prescription of spiritual disciplines or programs for spiritual development. Often material prosperity is promised in God's name if one gives an offering and plants seed money.

37. False teachers try to prevent Christians from enjoying the gifts of God. God has created these gifts and appointed them for our use. But the devil likes to contradict God and tempt people to hate His creation, even though God said it was good in Genesis 1:31. People are led to believe the problem of sin is in creation as a way of accusing the Creator God and justifying themselves. Alcohol, for example, is part of the natural creation and is to be used responsibly. But there are those who think that material objects are themselves sinful. They do not understand the Scriptures, such as Romans 14:14, "I know and am persuaded in the Lord Jesus that nothing is unclean in itself, but is unclean for anyone who thinks it is unclean." The same goes for all other institutions and orders of creation. Marriage is a divine institution and the standard social order for human life (Genesis 1:26; 2:15; Hebrews 13:4; Matthew 19:6). Likewise, food and eating are ordained by God and part of the created order for human life (see Genesis 1:29; 9:3; 1 Corinthians 10:31). All these things are good if received with prayer. Nothing is to be thrown aside as unfit for use.

38. 1 Timothy 4:2 describes the character of false teachers and verse 3 describes their teaching. These teachers attempt to erect another means of righteousness than that which God has provided in Christ through faith alone. They do this because they refuse to acknowledge their own sinfulness and that they cannot save themselves. Note Paul's strong language. He calls them deceivers, liars, and hypocrites, people who have defiled and hardened their consciences by means of their wicked teachings. Their very action of trying to gain righteousness and holiness through their own actions and not through faith alone reveals their consciences have been branded with guilt. They are desperately compensating for sin, since they have rejected God's grace and have done so because they refuse to accept the Law's verdict of their guilt. Consequently, they set up false standards of righteousness. Luther believed that this type of people have unnatural and dishonest consciences, and the things they proclaim as the highest wisdom and truth they in fact received from the devil (1 John 4:1–3).

The greatest danger that threatens the Church and all believers are false teachers. Note how often the apostle warns against false teachers in the Pastoral Epistles. In the course of time, deceivers have multiplied and the world is full of them today. Satan uses them to rob us of our faith and keep us from living the Christian life. Whoever lends an ear to them is in danger of falling away from Christ. The sad thing today is that false doctrines are not generally recognized as coming from the devil. The result is that these deceivers always succeed in drawing some church members into their nets.

39. A believer's faith can be nourished only by God's Word. He or she should therefore give his or her whole attention to true godliness, which concerns not stories, pious opinions, or even personal testimonies as such, but the person and work of Jesus Christ—the Gospel. Paul puts everything else on a level with the stories told by idle gossipers (1 Timothy 6:20; 2 Timothy 2:16; Titus 1:10, 14; 3:9). This applies also to all false doctrine and false teachers, as well as to the blatant errors of Mormonism, the Jehovah's Witnesses, and other cults.

40. Some people exert themselves to the limit in earthly contests but not in religion. Christians should not merely play at godliness. If faith is a priority with us, we will order and arrange our lives to see to it that spiritual interests and the concerns of eternity are placed ahead

of earthly ambitions and bodily desires. When we are preoccupied with health and beauty, spending vast amounts of time and resources to look and feel good while neglecting the growth of faith and edification of our souls, we show where our treasure really is.

41. To have some value means that physical exercise is profitable only to a certain extent. Training the body in temperate habits is of real advantage, and the Fifth Commandment requires that we take the best possible care of our bodies and health. That is part of the godly life. It is worth a great deal but not the main thing; it is little when compared with all that real godliness comprises. Paul does not disparage athletic exercises that are properly indulged in, but neither does he unduly exalt them as is done today (Colossians 2:18–23; Romans 13:14; 1 Timothy 5:23).

The word *godliness* means literally "good devotion." It refers to the proper or right devotion and reverence shown to God. As Lutherans, we know that the true worship of God does not consist in our works for Him but in believing and receiving His great work of salvation accomplished for us in Jesus Christ. To trust in Christ and make His action for us the focal point of our worship is to practice godliness. This results in a fruitful life of love and service to neighbor and abounds with true good works. Being right with God is both the basis and means of living the Christian life (Philippians 3:13–14), for by God's gracious forgiveness of our sins we are set free to do His will. True godliness is in the spirit, soul, heart, and life; it consists in faith, love, and all Christian virtues, the product of true Gospel preaching. The blessings of godliness do not end with this life; godliness has real value for time and eternity. It involves everything that pertains to the temporal and eternal welfare of our immortal souls, which is the idea of sanctification in the wide sense. God has given definite promises in regard to it (Romans 8:28; Mark 10:29–30; John 10:27–28; Revelation 14:13).

42. Timothy was not to let any critical attitude of people discourage him. He was probably between thirty-five and forty years of age and was not exactly a young man, since he had been Paul's assistant at least fourteen years. But some of the elders and members in Ephesus were considerably older and for that reason might question his authority. Paul did not consider Timothy too young to serve as his representative. In order to forestall criticism as much as possible, he said Timothy should exercise care and always set a good example

(Titus 2:7). The apostle specifies the following qualities: "in speech" (sound doctrine), "in conduct," "in love" (demonstrating grace to those who treat him rudely and disrespectfully), "in faith" (the confession of the Christian faith), and "in purity" (works of pure motives). 1 Timothy 4:13 directs Timothy to see to the public reading of the Scriptures in the church services. These were to be carefully selected, and no inappropriate remarks were to be allowed. Justin Martyr says that after the Scripture reading by the lector, a presbyter or some other person admonished and exhorted the people to take to heart what was read. An exhortation is an admonition to live by the Word, and teaching means strong doctrinal instruction.

43. 1 Timothy 4:14 refers to Timothy's ordination to the ministry. His special gift included the ability to understand and expound the Scriptures and to apply them. While all believers have the spiritual aptitude to comprehend the Word of God for themselves (Isaiah 54:13; John 6:45; 1 Thessalonians 4:9; 1 John 2:20–27), only those called to the pastoral office have the promise of ministerial grace to perform the work of shepherding God's people.

44. The pastor is Christ's chosen minister and gift to the congregation sent by Him to teach the Word of God. He is not a C.E.O., an emcee, or a visionary who devises grand schemes of institutional glory and inspires the people with them. Rather, he is Christ's shepherd sent to feed the flock the Gospel through Word and Sacrament. For it is through these means alone that Christ builds His Church.

45. In 1 Timothy 4:16, the Word of God says, "Keep a close watch on yourself and on the teaching. Persist in this, for by so doing you will save both yourself and your hearers." Please note that the pastor benefits hearers, those that humbly receive his ministry, and not those who proudly and arrogantly resist his ministry.

Lesson 6

Responsibilities Toward Others

Theme Verse: *But if anyone does not provide for his relatives, and especially for members of his household, he has denied the faith and is worse than an unbeliever.*

1 Timothy 5:8

Objectives

By the power of the Holy Spirit working through God's Word, we will:

- understand what opportunities a Christian has to serve his or her neighbor;
- desire to be of service to humankind;
- learn what God's will is in our treatment of pastors.

Some of our leading educators claim that people are living unhappy lives because they are not socially active or connected. They live too much for themselves and are not trying to fill their place in human society. The second table of the Law shows us how people are to live in community with others and work together for the common good. In our text, the apostle indicates how the Christian's attitude toward his or her neighbor works out in practice.

46. The apostle instructs Timothy on how to deal with individual members. The Christian Church is a great brotherhood. One must help and serve the other. We all still have our sinful flesh (Old Adam), which may lead us into sin. Christ has made it the duty of every Christian to admonish his fallen brother or sister (Matthew 18:15–20). Timothy is to show his people how to proceed when admonishing those who may need it. There is a certain respect due to age and rank and a certain wisdom necessary in dealing with young people. "Older

man" here means any older member, and in verse 17 it refers to pastors. The person who admonishes another should always be considerate and tactful. He or she should not act in a haughty, gruff, and superior manner or scold. When young people see older ones commit a sin, they should admonish them with due politeness and gentleness and speak to them as a loving child would talk to a parent who is at fault (Leviticus 19:32; Proverbs 16:32; 20:29). The relationship among Christians should be like that of a family. Those near the same age level should regard one another as brothers and sisters. All admonishing is to be without fault and in purity. The one who admonishes others must not be one who needs to be admonished.

47. The Church is not to be charged with the care of widows who have children or grandchildren that are able to support them. To aid one's parents is every Christian's duty. The Church must care for those who are left alone and helpless. The care of widows in the Early Church was a great problem (Acts 6:1–4). Widows in those days could find little opportunity for earning a living. 1 Timothy 5:5 describes a truly Christian widow. She sets her constant hope on God and lives a life of prayer and worship (Luke 2:37).

48. In 1 Timothy 5:8, Paul speaks to the specific needs of widows and the elderly from the general duty of gainful employment. Widows, together with all other dependents, belong to a family for all of whom the head of the house must provide. It is clearly implied that every person should try to fulfill his obligation by having an occupation and making an honest living. Besides supporting themselves, believers should also support those whom God has made dependent upon them: parents, if they can no longer take care of themselves, family, and other relatives who are in need. That is not charity but a Christian duty. Even non-Christians, as a rule, have enough feeling to provide for their relatives. One who neglects his or her dependents is worse than an unbeliever. Neglect of family members disregards the will of God and exhibits a life not ruled by faith.

49. In married life, the individual meets with fewer temptations to sin, which would bring reproach upon the Christian faith and cause offense to the world. By marrying a fellow believer, the Christian should find the ideal life. A woman is always blessed in the sphere of a Christian home. The home does not mean merely the physical space of a house but denotes the woman's life in relation to her husband and

children. In that position, she herself will be well taken care of, and she will also be able to help her needy relatives (1 Timothy 5:16).

50. In this section, the apostle again speaks of those who serve in the Church as pastors and teachers as "elders who rule well." First, Paul tells us how we should regard these men. Christians are to give their pastors special honor and should appreciate their service (1 Thessalonians 5:12–13; Hebrews 13:17). This means humbly, gratefully, and submissively receiving their ministry of the Gospel in faith. 1 Timothy 5:18 shows that this also includes paying them a fair salary, as something that congregations owe their pastors and teachers (1 Corinthians 9:11, 14; Galatians 6:6). Paul states this principle, which is already established in Deuteronomy 25:4 and mentioned in 1 Corinthians 9:9–11, which says, "You shall not muzzle the ox when it treads out the grain." And the second part of verse 18, "the laborer deserves his wages," is a word of Jesus recorded in Matthew 10:10 and Luke 10:7. In supporting their pastors properly, Christians show them honor and appreciation.

51. However, another way of showing our pastors honor is to think and speak well of them and shield their reputation. Satan tries to undermine their influence by causing evil reports to be raised against them. Unless these reports are well founded and can be verified by competent witnesses, church members should pay no attention to them. A person should always be considered innocent until it has been proven that he is guilty. Therefore, the Bible often demands that no accusation against any person is to be considered unless two or three witnesses can substantiate it (see Deuteronomy 19:15; Matthew 18:16; 2 Corinthians 13:1; Revelation 11:3). But if witnesses are able to prove the charges, then a guilty pastor is to be reprimanded publicly, as a warning to all other pastors. If he does not repent and remove the offense, the congregation is compelled to remove him from office. In such matters, no Christian should be swayed by partiality or favor. The integrity and honor of the office must be maintained. In performing his duties always as in the sight of God, the pastor will be charitable and fearless.

Lesson 7

Christian Stewardship

Theme verse: *But if we have food and clothing, with these we will be content.*

1 Timothy 6:8

Objectives

By the power of the Holy Spirit working through God's Word, we will:
- be encouraged to make faithful use of our talents and possessions as God's stewards;
- be content with the things God gives us to enjoy in this life;
- learn the value of true riches.

In Luke 12, Jesus tells the story of a rich man who was planning on building bigger barns to take care of his growing wealth and was thinking of the time when he could take life easy and enjoy his vast possessions. But what happened? "God said to him, 'Fool! This night your soul is required of you, and the things you have prepared, whose will they be?'" (Luke 12:20). Whether a Christian is poor or rich, Paul sets forth in today's session how we should regard and use the things of this world.

52. In 1 Timothy 6:1–2, Paul gives Timothy specific instructions in regard to slaves who had become Christians (Ephesians 6:5–10; Colossians 3:22–4:1; Titus 2:9–10). The Roman world was full of slaves, and we should remember that Roman slavery was quite unlike its counterpart in the Americas. "Under a yoke" brings out clearly what their condition was. They were like oxen under a yoke, driven by the will of their owner. While the Gospel does not forbid slavery, it does not encourage or abrogate it as a social institution either. Regardless of

our station, we should honor and obey those whom God has placed over us. This is because the Gospel is not the Law and as such concerns itself with God's gracious work of salvation in Jesus Christ. Certainly though, the Law speaks to this. But what does it say? The question must be very carefully answered because the issue is complex. Not all slaveries are the same. Practices of cruel subjugation and brutal oppression, such as experienced by countless Africans in Europe, the Americas, and in Africa itself, cannot be justified. Yet, as a social institution in ancient Rome, slavery permitted dignities and privileges to many slaves, many of whom were Northern Europeans. Many were well educated, and within slavery numerous subclasses and grades existed that involved slaves acting at nearly every level of society, in commerce, education, and government. But since being a free person or a slave has no bearing on one's salvation and the grace of God, and since Christ has redeemed all of life, slavery as a condition of life does not deprive a believer of any advantage or blessing from God. In fact, God's grace enables us to endure what is a very hard condition, because in and with us in all our toil and sufferings is Jesus Christ. In Christ, God humbled Himself to the lowest form of life, becoming a slave to perform the work of salvation for ungrateful people, enduring the cross, shame, indignity, and death. Therefore, those who find themselves in similar situations can submit in faith to God. This is how many early Christians bore witness for Christ. An excellent discussion may be found in John G. Nordling's commentary *Philemon* (St. Louis: Concordia Publishing House, 2004) on pages 39–139.

53. By faithfully practicing the teachings of Christianity in their lives, slaves would naturally make a good impression on their masters and perhaps even succeed in winning them for Christ. That was frequently the case in the Early Church. Many non-Christians realized that it was to their advantage when their servants became Christians. They were obedient, faithful, honest, and dependable. A Christian in such a position bears a heavy responsibility. Any wrong that he or she does will have an effect on his or her master and cause him or her to form a low opinion of the Christian religion. It may even move an unbeliever to revile Christ. Today, by means of our service, we should show forth the power of the Gospel. We should consider it a special privilege to work for Christian employers and under Christian supervisors.

54. The discussion of stewardship is often led along the lines of Law rather than Gospel. When this is done, the use or stewardship of time and talents has as its goal personal vindication or self-justification. One is always looking to be able to say he did the right thing and acted wisely so as to avoid being faulted, criticized, or accused. But as our Lord says, even when we have done "all that [we] were commanded," we must confess, "We are unworthy servants [literally slaves]; we have only done what was our duty" (Luke 17:10). However, when stewardship is thought of and practiced in view of the Gospel, it concerns itself with loving and serving and benefiting others. Here we do not look for earthly gains, profits, or increase for ourselves, believing if we get something out of an act or deed then it was good stewardship. Rather, we give away our lives, our goods, and all gain in this world, because God has in Christ secured for us eternal glory and riches in His kingdom. Thus, we are free to live in love. The use of time and treasure in love needs no justification since love fulfills the Law (Romans 10:13; Galatians 5:23).

55. The Christian religion also makes us rich insofar as it teaches us to be content with what we have and shields us from the dangers of a life of luxury and the love of money. Paul sounds a warning to all who want to be rich. One of the blessed fruits of faith is contentment. Godliness and contentment go together. A believer is satisfied with what God gives him or her of this world's goods, whether it be much or little. One who is content always has enough (Proverbs 30:8; Ecclesiastes 5:11–14; Psalm 37:16; Proverbs 13:11; 15:16; 16:8; 27:23, 24; Philippians 4:11–12, 18). Discontent is one of the greatest vices today. It is a foolish, dangerous, and sinful attitude of the heart. When a person is born into this world, he or she does not bring any earthly possessions with him or her (Job 1:21). Earthly possessions are transitory treasures of use only in this life, which itself is of short duration. We can take nothing along when we die (Psalm 49:16–17). What folly to set our hearts on earthly things (Luke 12:20–21)! Food, clothing and shelter are all that we really need.

56. The desire to be rich comes from an evil heart. This evil lust, or covetousness, begets a host of other sinful thoughts and deeds. Love of money and craving for more bring many temptations. A covetous person is tempted to ignore his or her neighbor's needs, to forsake him or her when in trouble, to defraud him or her, and to use sinful means for getting this world's goods. People usually enrich themselves at the

expense of others. Greed is a trap in which Satan ensnares the soul (Matthew 13:22; Mark 10:23–25). Faith cannot abide in such a heart. Numerous sins are the result of greed (e.g., dishonesty, bribes, lies, lawsuits, slander, jealousy, bribery, perjury, and murder). People who employ sinful means may get what they want, but they also get troubles and sorrows, the tortures of a bad conscience.

57. The believer's chief concern should be to cling to the Savior. Instead of reaching after worldly riches, he or she should guard against the sin of covetousness and seek the spiritual riches that God gives us in His Word. Note the sharp contrast between the person of the world and the child of God. The Christian should flee covetousness like a pestilence. Some people only pretend to flee. Believers should try to perfect themselves in every Christian virtue. Because of our sinful flesh, this is not easy. It requires a constant struggle with our sinful nature to be and remain a sanctified Christian. This is the fight of faith (2 Timothy 4:7; 1 Timothy 1:18). We must fight the enemies of our souls and defend our faith, for Satan seeks to destroy it (1 Peter 5:8–9). The Christian's equipment for warfare is described in Ephesians 6:13–17. The struggle is not in vain; the goal is eternal life, which we are not fighting to gain, of course, but to keep through faith alone.

58. Already in Baptism we are called to fight, to renounce the devil and sin. We do not know when Timothy made his good profession. Let us often think of the confession of faith that we made when we were baptized and confirmed. Through the Gospel, the Holy Spirit enables us to make this confession and live up to it. The Word makes us spiritually alive and constantly sustains the new life of faith. We should confess Christ before people, as He confessed the truth before Pilate (Matthew 27:11; John 18:37). The commandment that He has given us is the whole doctrine of salvation: the Gospel, and we are called to keep this faith.

Lesson 8

Be Not Ashamed of Your Faith

Theme Verse: *Therefore do not be ashamed of the testimony about our Lord, nor of me His prisoner, but share in suffering for the Gospel by the power of God.*

2 Timothy 1:8

Objectives

By the power of the Holy Spirit working through God's Word, we will:

- be grateful for godly parents;
- not be ashamed of our faith and of our Church;
- identify the ways in which the means of grace equip us to suffer for the Gospel.

This epistle has been called Paul's last will and testament for Timothy. The purpose of the letter is to express Paul's longing for Timothy's company and to strengthen him for that service that the apostle himself was no longer able to render to the cause of Christ. The letter is personal throughout and reveals the tenderness of a strong, loving, and heroic heart. The keynote of the epistle is "not ashamed," (2 Timothy 1:8, 12, 16). The whole letter throbs with the love of a father for a beloved child. Paul's work as an apostle was to publish the promise of eternal life in Christ. He had highest praise and deepest affection for his friend and helper. Sweet, blessed memories filled his heart as he was lying in prison awaiting his execution; gratefulness lifted him above all sadness. With a good conscience, the apostle was able to review his own past (v. 3). He and his ancestors had always believed in the promise of the Messiah and had zealously tried to live in obedience to the divine Law. He had been sincere even when he persecuted the Christians. Since his conversion, Paul had been serving God in true faith, like his Old Testament ancestors. His conscience as a believer was clean, even though Christianity was a forbidden religion in the Roman Empire. Paul was no longer able to preach the Gospel, but he did not spend the long nights and days in the dungeon in idleness. He spent much of his time in prayer, especially petitioning God to enable Timothy to continue his, the apostle's, work. Verse 4 expresses a personal reason for writing this letter (2 Timothy 4:9, 21). Paul's last wish was to see Timothy once more before his end. This reveals how strongly he was attached to the younger man. He could not forget the tears that Timothy had shed when he had left him at Ephesus to go either to Spain or to Rome. That was proof of loyal devotion to a spiritual father. The thought of seeing Timothy once more cheered the heart of the apostle.

59. Being raised in a Christian home is a privilege and gift from God. There God's name is feared and His promises believed. Under the influence of the Word of God, a pattern of reverence toward God and trust in His Word are established. Children have the great advantage of being reminded of God's grace in Christ given them in Baptism as a foundation for life. Timothy is an example. Since the days of his youth when he became a Christian, Timothy had conducted himself as a sincere and consecrated believer. His whole life had been a testimony of his faith (Philippians 2:20). He was a true spiritual son of Paul. His faith was like that of his mother, Eunice, and grandmother, Lois. Paul knew both women well and may have been instrumental in their conversion (Acts 16:1).

60. Knowing the Lord from early childhood means that one's personal, intellectual, and psychological developments take place under the influence of the Holy Spirit. The knowledge of God's Word is rooted in the mind and heart at the earliest stages of growth and affects a person for life. Young people should not be ashamed of the faith of their parents. The child's sense of identity is connected with Christ the Savior from the beginning of their consciousness. The character and the influence of godly parents are a power for good in the life of a young person. Blessed are the children that have such parents!

61. Because God hears and answers the prayers of His people, and because the "prayer of a righteous person has great power as it is working" (James 5:16), we may and should ask God's blessing upon

all whom we love. To remember them is to consider their lives of value to us.

62. Faith is sincere when it is the result of the Holy Spirit working through the Gospel to cause us to trust in Christ out of repentance for our sin. It is genuine when it is what we practice before God and not merely before men. Faith that is something we just put on like an act, as if we were just playing a part, and not what the Spirit produces in our hearts in the sight of God through the Gospel, is not sincere or true faith.

63. Paul was not ashamed of his faith. In connection with his suffering for the sake of the Gospel, Paul describes the glory of being a Christian (vv. 9–11). That we should become believers was settled in eternity (election, predestination). There was nothing in us that moved God to call us unto eternal life (2 Thessalonians 2:13). Salvation is only by grace; what God does for us during our earthly lives is to serve His purpose of love. This gracious purpose He has revealed to us in the Gospel. He planned and willed our salvation in eternity before He created the world (Ephesians 1:4, 11). Reflection on this brings joy because it fixes our thoughts not on the passing difficulties of this world but on the eternal blessings that God has promised to sinful people.

64. The Gospel is the light that shows what God has done for our salvation in Christ. It works in us spiritual life, preserves us from eternal death, and bestows upon us immortality and incorruption. The believer may at all times be certain of his or her salvation, since it is based upon Christ's work alone and since God, who cannot lie, has unconditionally promised it to us in this Word. The cross is the sign and guarantee of our salvation, and nothing can change the work it has accomplished.

65. This Gospel was the strength and support of Paul's faith. That is why neither sufferings nor dangers could shake his faith. The one purpose of his life had been to proclaim the Gospel to everyone. No matter what other people might do to him, he remained faithful to his calling as the apostle to the Gentiles. He was not ashamed to bear the disgrace of being a Christian. Wicked people cannot harm the Gospel. Paul knew the Christ whom he trusted and was convinced that Christ would guard the Gospel, so that its work would not be stopped. The Lord had placed, or deposited, His Gospel in the hands of Paul. After his death, it would be safely carried forward by others. In 2 Timothy

1:13–14, he calls upon Timothy to hold and guard this same deposit. This implies that God will also keep His elect in the faith unto the end.

66. Timothy's faith is to be centered in the Gospel, and he is never to forsake it. He is to use it faithfully in all his loving work of teaching and guiding others. Timothy's end is not yet in sight, as Paul's is. So he must guard his precious charge (1 Timothy 6:20). This will be safe as long as the Holy Spirit dwells in his heart, and the means of grace are that by which the Spirit is given and works in our lives. Through the means of grace alone—Word and Sacrament—and nothing else, does the Spirit grow us up in faith.

67. Professing Christians who are ashamed of fellow Christians are acting contrary to their claims of faith. 1 John 5:1 says that "everyone who loves the Father loves whomever has been born of Him." Sometimes we are tempted to be ashamed of Christians because of their weaknesses, humble status in life, or even their joy in the Lord. Ultimately, this is being ashamed of Christ Himself, who is unashamed to call us openly His brothers (Hebrews 2:11–12).

68. The love of God teaches us to put others ahead of ourselves and to value their welfare and lives more than our own. This is the nature of divine love. It enables us to do so because it first is given to us for the sake of Christ who died and atoned for our sins. This love is guaranteed to be ours for eternity and meets our deepest needs. Consequently, we are set free to act and live for others since God has brought us into His Fatherly care and love and promises to take care of all our needs, bear all our burdens, and deliver us from all our troubles.

69. The service of love is any act we perform in regard for others, because we have been so loved by God in Jesus Christ. We treat others and regard them as Christ has treated and regarded us. Though by nature we are sinful and unclean, through the cross and in Christ God has shown Himself friendly to us. In doing so, God regarded us as His own. When we do the same, we are emulating His love and God considers this to be service to Christ Himself.

70. Think especially of those who because of their situation, condition, circumstances, or problems might be forgotten or avoided by others. Think of the lonely, the sick, the elderly, and the least of people.

Lesson 9

Christian Warfare

Theme Verse: *Do your best to present yourself to God as one approved, a worker who has no need to be ashamed, rightly handling the word of truth.*

2 Timothy 2:15

Objectives

By the power of the Holy Spirit working through God's Word, we will:
- understand that the Christian life is constant warfare against sin and evil;
- understand that faith in Christ is the only way to victory;
- recognize the power and sufficiency of God's grace in Christ for conducting pastoral ministry and living the Christian life.

As Christians, we are citizens of Christ's kingdom, which is threatened by many enemies from within and without. These enemies seek to destroy our souls by separating us from Christ. As long as we live on earth, we must therefore be on our guard against them and not permit them to conquer us. The apostle shows how important it is that we fight as good soldiers of Jesus Christ.

71. In 2 Timothy 2:1–7, we have what Paul asks Timothy to be and to do. The chief thing a believer, and especially a pastor, needs is to be strong in the grace of Christ. God's grace is the source of all spiritual strength. What Timothy had been taught by Paul, he is to teach to others. And here he has in view the training of ministers in particular. They must be models of the grace of God, men who in all their weakness and powerlessness serve by God's favor and strength

97

gained for them in Christ. Their lives and ministry take the form of the cross, and therefore the source of power and the cause of the Gospel's fruitfulness are found only in God. Human plans and devices, however much they prove effectual outside the Church in the secular world, are not the divine instruments God makes use of to perform ministry.

Thus, the sound doctrine of the Gospel and the grace of God are to be preserved to the end of time. Note how important Paul considers Christian teaching; the Church is perpetuated only by means of teaching. Its doctrine not only brings people to faith but also fortifies them against the dangers that threaten their spiritual lives.

72. All believers on earth are members of the Church militant. Christ, the head of the Church, is the leader and captain. His subjects are the soldiers in His army. These are pitted against the forces of Satan. A soldier who refuses to fight for the cause of his general drops out of the ranks. A soldier is expected to remain loyal and fight to the finish. A soldier's life is not an easy life. He must endure all kinds of hardships, and therefore he has to become hardened to the requirements of army life. The soldier has to have the willingness and determination to fight on no matter what it costs. He must be willing to suffer and die for the cause. He must abstain from all things that will hinder him in the fight. His sole business is to do what he is told, to give a good account of himself as a fighter, and to let others provide for his needs.

This means hearing and believing the Gospel. For pastoral ministry, it means relying upon the weaponry of God's grace alone and not looking to human wisdom, resources, or means to do the will of God. The Gospel alone converts, sanctifies, and motivates people to lead God-pleasing lives. Pressure tactics—programs that use coercive measures or that recruit people through flattery or appeals to spiritual pride—are to be shunned by pastors. They must use the Gospel alone in their service and good fight.

Verse 5 adds the picture of an athlete. The training courses among the Greeks were very severe. To win a contest, a person must have himself under control and play the game according to the rules. How many run for a time and think they will secure the crown! But they run off the track of faith and love and thus, after all, lose the crown. This means that we live and minister by grace alone. We are exercised by it and through faith alone run the race in this world—not by our works of righteousness or great acts of spirituality. Verse 6 compares the believer to a farmer. The farmer works a long time before he sees the results of his labors and is not discouraged by the fact that the harvest is a good way off. In the end, he is sure to benefit by his labors. The believer's toil produces the fruits of godliness.

73. As stated in the previous question, the rule of pastoral ministry and Christian living is the Gospel or the grace of God in Christ. In the Church, or that which is called the kingdom of the right, God's gracious power is exercised and His saving work accomplished not through instruments that in the secular world—the kingdom of the left—are normally and naturally used. The Law is the rule of life in the secular world; the grace of God alone is the rule of life in the spiritual realm.

74. Union with Christ is accomplished through the means of grace alone accompanied by faith. The means of grace are the conferring instruments through which God acts and faith is the receiving instrument through which people respond. Faith is God's gift and is itself created by the Gospel. This union is solely based upon Christ's incarnation and atonement. He has made Himself one with us and taken our sin to the cross and thus enabled us to be made one with Him. By this union we are granted eternal life, the Holy Spirit, fellowship with God, the indwelling of the Holy Trinity, the guardianship of elect angels, and grace to endure all trials through which we may pass in this life.

75. The two chief doctrines in Scripture are the Law and the Gospel. Briefly, the Formula of Concord explains the difference as follows: "We believe, teach, and confess that the Law is properly a divine doctrine (Romans 7:12). It teaches what is right and pleasing to God, and it rebukes everything that is sin and contrary to God's will. For this reason, then, everything that rebukes sin is, and belongs to, the preaching of the Law. But the Gospel is properly the kind of teaching that shows what a person who has not kept the Law (and therefore is condemned by it) is to believe. It teaches that Christ has paid for and made satisfaction for all sins (Romans 5:9). Christ has gained and acquired for an individual—without any of his own merit—forgiveness of sins, righteousness that avails before God, and eternal life (Romans 5:10)" (FC Ep V 3–5). A recommended resource for further study is *God's No and God's Yes* (St. Louis: Concordia Publishing House, 1973). It is a condensed version of C.F.W. Walther's book *The Proper Distinction Between Law and Gospel.*

The right application consists in preaching the Law only to put to death the Old Adam in us and to produce repentance. It is not a means of justification or sanctification. The right application also consists in preaching the Gospel only to raise men up to life and faith. It is not a means of condemnation but of justification and sanctification. The Law is God's command and speaks of works that we must do. The Gospel is God's promise and speaks only of the work that He has done for us in Christ that saves us from wrath and gives to us all the riches of heaven freely for Christ's sake.

76. Outward membership in the Church does not make one a child of God. The believers are the gold and silver vessels in God's house. The hypocrites, vessels of wood and earth, are worthless members to be discarded (Matthew 13:47–50; 7:22–23). The former honor and the latter dishonor God. Only believers are precious in God's sight. These must keep themselves clean in doctrine and life, live a sanctified life, remain fit to serve their Master, and be fruitful in good works. Here there is a distinct emphasis on separation from false doctrine and false teachers. Life follows doctrine, and where doctrine is corrupt, life will be also.

77. In order to be a vessel that is precious and useful to God, the believer should avoid sinful desires and lusts that war against the soul. Each age of life has its own temptations. Youthful passions are particularly dangerous, because if they are not suppressed they may gain control over one's whole life. The strongest antidote against evil tendencies and habits is growth in the Christian virtues (2 Timothy 2:22).

Lesson 10

The Believer's Security in an Evil World

Theme Verse: *From childhood you have been acquainted with the sacred writings, which are able to make you wise for salvation through faith in Christ Jesus.*

2 Timothy 3:15

Objectives

By the power of the Holy Spirit working through God's Word, we will:
- become aware of the influence of sin in the Church and how it affects our lives;
- understand how necessary it is for Christians to have a sound knowledge of the Scriptures in order to resist the evil in the world, remain in faith, and serve God with good works;
- gain awareness of the threat of false doctrine.

The world today likes to boast of its wisdom and accomplishments, as though it were superior to all previous generations. But how easily people are deceived by foolish ideas and led astray by religious quacks! Paul shows to what low levels people sink when they reject the grace of God. The words of our text are a warning to us to be more faithful in the use of God's Word lest we also should be deceived by the pretensions of the ungodly.

78. As Paul's life was drawing to a close, it was natural for him to become deeply concerned about the Church of the future. God granted him some glimpses into the future so that he could warn the believers of dangers they would encounter in the course of time (2 Thessalonians

2:3; 1 Timothy 4:1–3; Matthew 24:11–12). By divine revelation, Paul knew that the Church would face perilous times and that conditions in the world would get worse the nearer Judgment Day approached. The increase of wickedness in the world would endanger the faith of believers, and weak Christians would be tempted to adopt the sinful ways of the ungodly. Paul wanted to fortify believers against this danger. Therefore, he painted a dark but true picture of a Christless world. It should be interesting for us to note how much people of today resemble those whom the apostle describes.

79. What is wrong with the world today? Selfishness is the cause of much of the world's troubles. "For people will be lovers of self" (2 Timothy 3:2). Many people are concerned only about themselves and their own interests. That makes them covetous, money-mad, greedy, and dishonest. How little reverence one finds for sacred things! People prefer to be unholy and impure, stained with all kinds of sins. They do not even love their closest relatives, as may be seen in many homes and in divorce courts. *Unappeasable* means that they are disagreeable in every way and impossible to satisfy. Slanderers think only of gossip, accusation, and blackmailing. Those without self-control cannot be held in check; they are bound to get what they want. When they are opposed, they show a brutal temper, and they thoroughly hate those who try to live clean and upright lives. Those who are treacherous are not faithful to their own country or even to their own friends. The reckless are headstrong and stubborn in having their own way. Others are swollen with conceit and are haughty; they like to put on airs (Romans 1:29–32; Jude 16; 2 Peter 2:12). Who will deny that the world is pleasure-mad and that even some church members care much more about being entertained and a good time than about God? Many who are outwardly connected with the Church live as sinfully as unbelievers. What a frightful picture of our own age! These conditions are a challenge to our Church to keep itself unspotted by the world and to apply the only remedy (Matthew 5:13–14).

80. 2 Timothy 3:6 reminds us of the practices of proselyting cults (e.g., the Mormons, the Jehovah's Witnesses, and others) who go from house to house and by their tracts and slick talk seek to win unstable people for their cause. Those who are idle and foolish, whose only object in life is pleasure, are their easy victims. These deceivers creep around, trying to hide from the watchful eyes of Christian pastors. False teachers have used the media—radio, television, the Internet,

tapes, books, CDs, and other forms of communication—to undermine homes and to counteract the influence of God's Word. Satan's agents succeed especially with those who are weak in the faith, looking for some doctrine that will permit them to sin in security, or with such as have never had a foundation of sound Christian knowledge (v. 7).

All people are potential victims of false teaching. However, today women are especially targeted by so-called Bible teachers on the radio, television, Internet, and even the Christian bookstore. They claim to be ministering to the body of Christ, but they are improperly doing the work of the ministry and supplanting pastors. Christ has not called them to perform this work but has established the Church and the pastoral office to minister the Word of God.

81. There are two main reasons for the acceptance of error by people. To begin with, people are born spiritually blind and lack any ability to discern truth from error. They can be made to believe anything since they are devoid of the knowledge of the truth. The other cause is much worse. This occurs because people turn from the truth. Such people have been illuminated by the Holy Spirit through the Word of God. But instead of remaining true to the faith, they become discontented and seek after what will satisfy their carnal and sinful desires.

82. Christians are most certainly persecuted today. Islamic countries and repressive governments such as North Korea, China, the Sudan, and Cuba persecute believers. Also, in some countries where Roman Catholicism is dominant, priests and other church officials stir up fear among local people, and they spread rumors and make slanderous charges against evangelical Christians. They resist the truth of God's Word and are disqualified regarding the faith; they will not stand the test with regard to the true faith.

83. The world manifests its hatred of Christians in many ways. They accuse, slander, and ridicule them, and they try to do them harm. They oppose their doctrine and mischaracterize the Christian faith in order to prejudice others. The apostle Paul was not popular with the world. From the time he became a Christian, he had to endure the hatred of the ungodly. Timothy had witnessed some of this in and near his old hometown of Lystra (Acts 13:50; 14:5, 19).

84. It is not unusual for those who profess faith in Christ and live up to their convictions to be disliked and even persecuted by the world. Christians need not fear persecutions and afflictions. By such trials, the

Church has often been purified and made strong. The only real danger from without is heresy or false doctrine. False teachers are seducers, cheats, who first deceive others and finally believe their own lies. Believers must constantly be on their guard against them.

85. Verse 15 states that Timothy had been acquainted with God's Word since infancy. Doubtless this means that he was raised in a home where his mother and grandmother exposed him to the Scriptures from birth. It is clear that their teaching of Timothy was not a case of saying one thing and doing another. Paul calls their faith "sincere" (2 Timothy 1:5). Much good teaching done by parents is undone by inconsistent and hypocritical lives.

86. In 2 Timothy 3:14, Timothy is told to "continue in what you have learned and have firmly believed." Christians should continue through life in the things they have learned from God's Word. How often is it the case that, after confirmation, people become lax in their attention to God's Word?

87. The Bible is different in that it is the very Word of God. It is said to be "breathed out from God" (v. 16). This means these words originate from God and are first and fundamentally His. The Bible alone is God's inspired Word.

88. Some people are particularly anxious to overthrow the doctrine of inspiration. Why? To them the Bible is only a human book that people may interpret as they wish. What the Bible claims for itself is not a theory of inspiration but a plain and fundamental doctrine. The Bible does not contain the ideas or words of men, but is God-breathed. Every word in it is divine truth. It can contain no mistakes and no errors, because God cannot lie. And it proves itself to us in its work in our lives. Its fundamental purpose is to make us wise unto salvation by bringing us to faith in Christ. It accomplishes this purpose in a fourfold manner: (1) by teaching the truth regarding God and heavenly things and imparting the facts connected with our salvation (teaching); (2) by pointing out what is false and dangerous to the soul (reproof); (3) by helping the believer correct his or her faults and amend his or her ways in accordance with God's Law (correction); and (4) by leading to godliness, growth in holiness (training in righteousness). "Worldly wisdom and righteousness, which may be acquired from other books, can never create the man of God or indoctrinate. This can be accomplished solely by the Holy Scriptures, which are inspired and given by God" (Luther).

89. Verbal and plenary inspiration are necessary not only because the Scriptures teach this, but also because to deny this is to put the Bible's authority and infallibility in doubt. Faith in God's Word is undermined and occasion is given to people to sit in judgment of God's Word when this is denied or questioned in any way.

Lesson 11

The Reward of a Godly Life

Theme Verse: *I have fought the good fight, I have finished the race, I have kept the faith. Henceforth there is laid up for me the crown of righteousness.*

2 Timothy 4:7, 8

Objectives

By the power of the Holy Spirit working through God's Word, we will:

- keep the final goal of the Christian life in mind, so that this may spur us on to greater faithfulness in the service of the Lord;
- consider how God enables us to keep the faith;
- gain assurance of God's promise of eternal life.

Some people dislike to be reminded of death, and they carefully avoid this topic. But death is a thing that no child of God needs to fear, because for him or her it is merely the passing out of this world into heaven. For this reason, men and women of strong faith joyfully look forward to the end of their lives. We see from their statements how eager some of them have been to go to their eternal home when on their deathbed. Many of these have been written down and preserved, such as Luther's last words, which were reportedly: "O heavenly Father, if I leave this body and depart, I am certain that I shall be with Thee forever and can never tear myself out of Thy hands. Father, into Thy hands I commend my spirit. Thou hast redeemed me, Thou faithful God." President Andrew Jackson said as he was dying: "I am ready to depart. Upon the Bible I rest my hope for eternal salvation."

Many of the last words of believers are like the sentiment expressed by Simeon (Luke 2:29). In this lesson we will examine the last words that Paul wrote and in which he gives expression to his feelings and thoughts as he realized that his end was near.

Paul closes his last letter with an appeal to Timothy to remain faithful to his God-given charge. Together with Timothy, Paul stands before the judgment throne of God, charging his beloved disciple to preach the Word. He reminds Timothy that on Judgment Day he will have to give an account of his stewardship. His whole duty as a pastor is stated in three words: "Preach the Word." God does not leave it to human beings to decide when His Word is to be proclaimed, because then it would not be done. A pastor should be ready for every opportunity of preaching: in the regular services, on special occasions, in public, and in private. People should have opportunity to hear the Gospel whether they care to listen or not. The Church must make every effort to obtain a hearing for its message.

90. The most useful lives we can live and the best service we can render our neighbor is to guard faithfully our spiritual treasures, not let the hardships that we must suffer as Christians discourage us, and live lives of faith in Christ and love to neighbor that testify of God's saving grace. When our lives have been led in this way, they will be useful and fruitful in God's kingdom.

91. The whole Church is the possessor of the keys (Matthew 16:19; 18:18–20). Jesus' mandate to make disciples is given to the whole Church (Matthew 28:19, 20). Although the work of baptizing and teaching all things is the work of public ministry and is ordinarily carried out by pastors, all believers are responsible to see to it that this is done. Therefore, they are to call and ordain pastors. In addition, they themselves are called to be lights in a dark world and hold forth the Gospel to unbelievers (Philippians 2:15–16).

92. The sinner's opportunity is the time when God offers His grace. If this is put off to some future time, it may be too late (Acts 25:25; 2 Corinthians 6:2). The Word is to be applied as the hearer needs it. Sinners are to be reproved and convinced of their sins. The indifferent are to be rebuked and warned of God's judgment.

93. We have here the remarkable words of confidence and triumph that only a child of God can utter. They show us how a believer, standing at the end of life's journey, views both his or her past and future. Paul lets us know how he felt when his life was

drawing to a close. The prospect of death did not fill his heart with dismay and terror but with holy joy and confident exultation. His whole life as a Christian had been spent in that spirit (Philippians 1:20–23). He considers his death as a final offering up of himself to God, like the pouring out of a drink offering (Numbers 15:1–10; Philippians 2:17; Romans 15:16). Like a pilgrim on the way home, he is about to break up camp for the last time. He is to leave this world, and he is ready to go. He knows that better things are beyond. He has no regrets as to his past. The wrongs he had done or suffered are forgiven and forgotten. Looking back, he pictures his life as a fight and a contest or race he has run. Both pictures were true to life. His life had been a conflict, at times most bitter and painful. How much suffering Satan and wicked men had caused him! What difficulties, dangers, and hardships he had been obliged to face! But now it was almost over; he had won the victory and reached the goal. He had kept his faith and had finished the work the Lord had called him to do. He had fought to keep the Gospel pure and had defended it against all heretics. 2 Timothy 4:7 is the victor's exulting shout. His ship of life was ready to be loosed from its moorings that it might speed to the harbor of eternal rest (Philippians 3:12–17).

94. Now Paul looks ahead (2 Timothy 4:8). He knows that the prize, the reward of victory, is ready and waiting for him. It is worth all the struggle and effort, all the suffering and sacrifice (Romans 8:18). He gives all glory to God who had accomplished this through him. What wonderful words of hope and assurance that he can lay claim to a crown of eternal blessedness! God has reserved for him a crown of righteousness, which is for all who remain faithful to Christ. Elsewhere it is called a "crown of life" and "a crown of glory" (James 1:12; 1 Peter 5:4). This crown is God's reward of grace promised to all believers (Revelation 7:15; 1 Peter 1:4–5; Psalm 17:15). It consists in perfect sinlessness and all the blessings that are to be ours in the life beyond the grave. Paul here is not thinking of special honors and glory that God will bestow upon those who were most faithful in His service. In heaven there will indeed be degrees of glory (2 Corinthians 9:6; Daniel 12:3). Who would not wish to be able to die like Paul? Only believers are prepared to leave this world with such a joyful and triumphant faith. They look anxiously forward to the coming of their Lord to take them home to heaven.

95. Paul still had to get over a few more hard places before he would reach his goal. His last wish that he hoped to see fulfilled before his end was to see Timothy once more. He, therefore, urged his friend to hasten to Rome as quickly as possible (2 Timothy 4:21). There was still much that he wished to tell Timothy, whom he was leaving behind to take his place. How fond he was of his faithful helper, and how highly he thought of him! But there were some who saddened the closing days of the aging apostle. Demas at one time had received favorable mention (Colossians 4:14). But he showed himself weak when the test came and hurriedly withdrew from Paul when he was threatened with persecution. Love for the world drew him away from Christ.

96. Paul requested Timothy to bring John Mark with him to Rome. The apostle had by this time changed his opinion about Mark (Acts 15:38). Mark reminds us that God's grace, and not our failures or weaknesses, determines our service and usefulness for Him.

Paul wished to have his cloak, which he had left at Troas, probably because he was now being kept in a cold cell. What the books and parchments (manuscripts) were we do not know. They may have been Paul's own copy of the Scriptures. Paul informed Timothy that his case had come up for its first hearing before the imperial court. It grieved him that no one volunteered to speak in his behalf. But the apostle bore all disappointments and wrong with noble Christian fortitude and prayed that God would forgive his false friends. He had learned during the years of his ministry not to rely too strongly on people. But he knew that God was with him. The Lord made His presence known to Paul and gave him the strength and comfort he needed. Through his testimony before the emperor, Paul was now crowning his past labors among the Gentiles. "Delivered from the lion's mouth" is a figurative expression meaning escape from mortal danger (Psalm 22:22; 35:17). As a Roman citizen, Paul would not be cast to the lions. His first trial resulted neither in condemnation nor acquittal. The court decided to postpone sentencing or to give the case a second hearing. Paul had no hope of being released. He knew that his end would come soon, but that would mean deliverance from all the evil of this world, which is an echo of the Seventh Petition. Martyrdom would merely open to him the gates of paradise. His soul was filled with hope and joy and sang praise to God. Paul's letters are filled with doxologies, and it is but natural that his last epistle should close with a hymn of praise and with an emphatic "Amen." These words of Paul show that, when a believer dies, his soul immediately goes to heaven (Philippians 1:21). The last words from the pen of Paul are a benediction. Paul disappears from history with a ringing cry of confidence and blessing. "But at evening time there shall be light" (Zechariah 14:7).

97. 2 Timothy 4:18 assures us that God's saving power may always be trusted in to grant deliverance to His children and servants. In every situation, especially those in which it appears sin and evil people have the upper hand and cannot be overcome, Christ stands over them victoriously working His good and gracious will in and through all things. This is what we pray for in the Seventh Petition of the Lord's Prayer when we ask God to "deliver us from evil." This means we are asking God not to exempt us from all suffering, but that the wicked plans and intentions of the devil will not prevail. Sin and the devil have designs to destroy and damn us. God's promise given to us in Christ is that He will work to realize His good and gracious purpose in those very works. The devil means it for ill; God means it for good.

Lesson 12

A Summary of the Christian Life

Theme Verse: *... showing all good faith, so that in everything they may adorn the doctrine of God our Savior.*

Titus 2:10

Objectives

By the power of the Holy Spirit working through God's Word, we will:

- thoroughly absorb Paul's instructions in the Pastoral Epistles pertaining to the Christian life;
- appreciate once again the teaching ministry of Christian pastors;
- recognize the threat of false and impure doctrine.

Last week we completed our study of Paul's epistles to Timothy. How much valuable information these two letters contain! They were a great help for increasing our knowledge of Christian doctrine and for showing us how Christians should live in this world. God wants to have these important truths impressed deeply upon our minds, so that we may always remember them and live according to them. Therefore, He has caused these matters to be stated again and again in the Scriptures but always in a somewhat different form and in an interesting manner. The Epistle to Titus offers us a splendid opportunity for reviewing what we have learned in the other two epistles.

The last two sessions of this Bible study have been planned to take the place of a usual review. The Epistle to Titus will serve well for this purpose. By reading the epistle and noting its outline and topics and comparing its content with that of the letters to Timothy, participants will not only become acquainted with this particular epistle but will be given a new opportunity for recalling and restudying from a different angle what has already been presented and discussed in previous sessions. The leader should make as much use as possible of parallel passages.

98. As was pointed out in Lesson 1, the Epistle to Titus was written at about the same time as the First Epistle to Timothy, which was AD 64 or 65. With the exception of the Epistle to the Romans, the Letter to Titus has a longer introduction than any other letter of Paul. In it, Paul affirms the commission of Titus to preach the Gospel and administer the Sacraments among the people in Crete. The case was different in Ephesus, where Paul and Timothy were well known. Crete was a new field, and since Paul had been there only a short time, the knowledge of the Cretan Christians was imperfect. The apostle had, therefore, left Titus behind as his representative. Whoever refused to heed Titus thereby refused to heed the apostle himself. Moreover, Paul is speaking to the Cretans by divine authority as a servant of God, one who is carrying out the Lord's will. This same Word of God that Paul and Titus were commissioned to preach gives divine authority to all Christian pastors and should command the attention and obedience of their hearers.

99. Because the Word of God is the principal means of grace, and because doctrine is nothing but that Word set forth in an organized and detailed manner, it is through doctrine that God's grace is delivered to believers. Their spiritual health is dependent upon the public ministry of the Word of God. Because Christ has instituted the public ministry to perform this service, the Christian pastor should be well trained in the teachings of the Bible so that he will be able to expose and refute any false teacher who endangers the faith of his flock. For just as good and sound doctrine produces healthy Christians and edifies faith, so false doctrine destroys faith and spiritually ruins the lives of men.

100. In verses 10–16, Paul stresses the necessity of keeping the congregations free from the influence of false teachers. Jewish errorists were particularly active on the isle of Crete; their chief interest was to enrich themselves by deceiving the gullible people. The Cretans had a bad reputation; they were known to be an unruly lot, disputing for the sake of controversy about unprofitable questions, fickle, dishonest, and

lazy. Paul quotes Epimenides, a poet of Crete, as one who did not trust his own people. Paul made use of every available means to learn about the habits and needs of the people whom he tried to serve. He knew that God's Word was the only means whereby the lives of these Cretans could be changed for the better. He gave Titus instruction to preach the Law of God in all its severity, so that these people might be brought to repentance. Titus was to urge the Cretans to break away from the useless traditions of the Jewish rabbis and from their commandments, which they added to the Old Testament, forbidding what God had permitted. Paul characterized the false teachers as impure persons who found some evil use for all of God's gifts (1 Timothy 4:3–4). They professed a profound knowledge of God's Word, but they were perverted in their teaching and abominable in their moral lives.

101. Paul now gives Titus pastoral advice, telling him how to deal with various kinds of people. All the instruction that a pastor gives to his members must be based on the sound doctrine of the Scriptures. All Christians are to be sober-minded, sound and balanced in judgment, and exercising complete self-control. Men of mature years should show qualities of ripened experience and give evidence that they have made good progress in Christian knowledge and sanctification. Older women should be good examples to the young women. Drunkenness was a widespread vice in all ages. The younger women should be trained to become good wives and mothers, if married.

102. We owe both our employers and supervisors respect and obedience. This we may do since we serve Christ and not people.

Lesson 13

A Summary of the Christian Faith

Theme Verse: *. . . waiting for . . . our great God and Savior Jesus Christ, who gave Himself for us to redeem us from all lawlessness and to purify for Himself a people for His own possession who are zealous for good works.*

Titus 2:13–14

Objectives

By the power of the Holy Spirit working through God's Word, we will:

- understand the importance of a sound knowledge of Christian doctrine for our faith and life;
- confirm our belief in holy Baptism as a true and powerful instrument of salvation;
- be encouraged to support the work of pastoral ministry.

Some people insist that the Church should stop teaching doctrines and should devote all its efforts to improving the morals of the world. Others want all religious teachings to be regarded as useful for developing humanity's spiritual life, even if they are not in agreement with the Bible. Finally, there are persons who are very zealous in keeping the doctrines of the Church pure from error but show no concern as to whether the church members are living in accordance with the teachings of the Scriptures. From our study of the Pastoral Epistles, it should have become clear to us that these current attitudes toward faith are wrong and dangerous. We have seen that the apostle considers the teachings of the Bible to be very important. He wants them to be kept pure from all human additions and perversions, and he regards them as having a direct and powerful bearing on the lives of those who believe these doctrines. In our final lesson, we will note that the Pastoral Epistles are a real treasure house of Christian doctrine.

In the second part of this Letter, Paul gives special prominence to the doctrines of justification and regeneration. The leader may show that in regard to both of these doctrines there is much error and confusion in the heterodox churches today.

A heterodox church is one that teaches the Gospel and the doctrines of Scripture impurely. It will not be possible to treat exhaustively the rich doctrinal content of the text, but the leader should mention that even the ancient Christian Church was so impressed with its beauty and value that it designated a part of this text to be read during the Christmas season.

103. The Gospel instructs and impels the believer to godliness. Paul shows what should induce us to live a sanctified life to the glory of our Savior and from where we obtain the strength and willingness to do so. The Gospel causes the believer to recognize worldly lusts as sinful and inconsistent with his faith. It gives the Christian a new viewpoint on life and clear and sound judgment in regard to spiritual matters. Note how often Paul uses the words *sober-minded* or *self-controlled* in Titus 2 (vv. 2, 4, 6, 12). The believer lives upright in his or her relation to other people and godly in relation to God. The believer's faith is to be adorned with good works. He or she is to live as a citizen of heaven, who has no continuing city on earth but waits longingly for the life to come. The believer looks forward to the time when he or she will forever be with the Lord (Revelation 22:17, 20). If this is our hope, then we will gladly deny ungodliness and all sins that would destroy our faith. Titus 2:14 expresses another reason for living a holy life. Christ gave Himself to free us from the bondage of sin. He purchased us to be His own and purified us from sin, to live as His own in His heavenly kingdom. (See Luther's explanation of the Second Article.)

104. These are the truths that Titus and all pastors are to teach in the Church and that all believers are to receive as God's own message to them, even though they are proclaimed by human lips (Luke 10:16; 1 Timothy 4:12).

105. Christians are to be constantly reminded that they should live in accordance with the divine truths, which they profess to believe.

They should prove themselves to be loyal and patriotic citizens and show proper respect for their government (Romans 13:1–8; 1 Timothy 2:1–2). They should always be ready to promote the welfare of their country and its citizens. Instead of having a quarrelsome disposition, believers should be yielding, considerate, and not insist on their own rights but be forbearing and kind toward all people. Our past sins and the fact that we are by nature no better than others should move us to be lenient with our neighbor. The old Adam in Christians is no different from that of non-Christians. It is the fallen, sinful nature that they fight against by the power of the Holy Spirit whose grace imparts to them a new nature.

106. The new birth is necessitated by the fact of human sinfulness. As Jesus said, "That which is born of the flesh is flesh, and that which is born of the Spirit is spirit" (John 3:6). People cannot by any act of their will or through any good deed bring this about. Only God, working through the Gospel, can do so.

107. God's infinite love is revealed in Christ's work of redemption. Salvation is by grace alone; we could not earn it by our works. It is altogether the result of God's love, kindness, mercy, and grace. All that Jesus has accomplished by His life and death God gives and seals to man by means of Holy Baptism.

108. Paul points to the "washing of regeneration and renewal of the Holy Spirit" (Titus 3:5) as that through which Christ's work of justification is personally applied to us and we are made heirs of eternal life. The word *washing* refers to a laver (a basin used in temple worship) or the washing done at one. There is only one instituted rite and act of ministry that makes use of water; it is Baptism. This Sacrament is not a mere rite or symbol but a means of grace through which the Holy Spirit works faith and regenerates the heart of a person. Far from being an argument against infant Baptism, it serves to justify it. Since the basis of salvation is found not in our works or actions but God's alone, children, who are capable of virtually nothing, can also be saved through these waters. Since God's work and promise of salvation in Christ are for all people and not adults only, infants may and should (and must!) be baptized for their salvation.

109. In his Small Catechism, Luther says that Baptism "works forgiveness of sins, rescues from death and the devil, and gives eternal salvation to all who believe this, as the words and promises of God declare." Our Baptism assures us of our justification before God,

bestows upon us the blessings of Christ's redemption, makes us heirs of salvation, and gives us the hope of eternal life.

110. Paul closes his doctrinal instruction with his favorite expression, "This saying is trustworthy," absolutely reliable. The phrase is like an emphatic "Amen." The apostle states emphatically that Christianity is not merely a matter of the head and intellect but of the heart and life. It is a practical religion. The Gospel is to be preached to believers as long as they live, in order that they may grow in knowledge and sanctification (2 Peter 3:18). By living according to the Gospel, people will derive inestimable benefits for themselves and will be most profitable to their neighbor.

111. The Gospel also enlightens and strengthens them, so that they will not fall prey to religious deceivers but know how to deal with them. Paul was not a man to compromise with fanatics and errorists. How often he warns the believers in the Pastoral Epistles to guard against human speculations, religious trash, and false doctrines, which endanger a Christian's faith! The Church should properly admonish heretics and in brotherly love try to lead them to a knowledge of the truth. But if they refuse to become convinced and continue in their error, they should not be permitted to hold membership in the Church (Romans 16:17; 1 John 4:1). To believe and to teach a false doctrine are grievous sins, which, if not repented of and forsaken, will lead the deluded person into perdition.

112. Paul said that Christians are under obligation to preach the Gospel to all people (Romans 1:14). Though not all are called to public ministry, to teach and preach and rightly administer the Sacraments, all are called to be witnesses. Christians are called to speak God's Word in their daily life. This also means sacrificing our time to pray for, and our treasures to pay for, the work of the Gospel. Titus was to urge the Cretans to give these missionaries the necessary support. The new congregations needed to be trained to participate in the work of the Church at large.